PERCEPTUAL ADJUSTMENT THERAPY

PERCEPTUAL ADJUSTMENT THERAPY

A Positive Approach
to Addictions Treatment

James Holder III, LPC, NCAC II
with
Thurman Williams III

ACCELERATED DEVELOPMENT
A member of the Taylor & Francis Group

USA	Publishing Office:	ACCELERATED DEVELOPMENT
		A member of the Taylor & Francis Group
		1101 Vermont Ave., N.W., Suite 200
		Washington, DC 20005
		Tel: (202) 289-2174
		Fax: (202) 289-3665
	Distribution Center:	ACCELERATED DEVELOPMENT
		A member of the Taylor & Francis Group
		1900 Frost Road, Suite 101
		Bristol, PA 19007-1598
		Tel: (215) 785-5800
		Fax: (215) 785-5515
UK		Taylor & Francis, Ltd.
		4 John Street
		London WC1N 2ET
		Tel: 071 405 2237
		Fax: 071 831 2035

PERCEPTUAL ADJUSTMENT THERAPY: A Positive Approach to Addictions Treatment

1 2 3 4 5 6 7 8 9 0 BRBR 0 9 8 7 6 5

This book was set in Times Roman by Sandra F. Watts. Technical development by Cynthia Long. Artwork in Figure 7.1 by Susan Arnold. Cover design by Michelle Fleitz. Printing and binding by Braun-Brumfield, Inc.

A CIP catalog record for this book is available from the British Library.

∞ The paper in this publication meets the requirements of the ANSI Standard Z39.48-1984 (Permanence of Paper)

Library of Congress Cataloging-in-Publication Data
Holder, James.
    Perceptual adjustment therapy: a positive approach to addictions treatment/James Holder III, with Thurman Williams III.
        p. cm.
    Includes bibliographical references and index.

    1. Compulsive behavior—Treatment. 2. Substance abuse—Treatment. I. Williams, Thurman. II. Title.
[DNLM: 1. Behavior, Addictive—therapy. 2. Psychotherapy—methods. WM 176 H727p 1995]
RC533.H65 1995
616.86 ' 0651—dc20
DNLM/DLC
for Library of Congress   95-14249
                                                                      CIP

ISBN 1-56032-393-0

TABLE OF CONTENTS

LIST OF FIGURES

ACKNOWLEDGEMENTS

I would like to offer special thanks to the faculty and staff at West Virginia University's Department of Counseling and Rehabilitation, especially Dr. Mike Yura for his introduction to Adlerian psychology and family therapy. I am also grateful to Dr. Frank Walton, Dr. Don Dinkmeyer, and the Adlerian Psychological Association in South Carolina for their support through the years.

I also would like to thank Julian Silverman and Richard Price at Esalen Institute for our wonderful Gestalt experiences, and for their interpretations of experiences with Fritz Perls. Dr. John Mulgrew has shared with me many joyful and tearful years of friendship in Gestalt therapy, and Gregory Bateson at Esalen Institute provided for me a spiritual connection and underpinning for all therapy.

John Grinder and the Neuro-Linguistic Program trainers brought the structure of excellence into my conscious awareness, and for that I will always remain grateful.

In addition to directly contributing to the work that follows, my wife Rosie has been an enduring support, a careful editor, a stirring motivator, and the finest addictions counselor I have ever known.

Finally I would like to thank Joe Hollis and everyone at Accelerated Development and Taylor & Francis for their patience and support.

Without all of these people and their many contributions, none of this would have been possible.

DEDICATION

To Jim, Nell, and Albert. For giving me the strength, compassion, and love to work with those pained from addictions.

PREFACE

This was an accident. I didn't set out to create a new therapy for addictions treatment; instead, it seems more like Perceptual Adjustment Therapy happened to me. Professionally, I followed a very typical counseling path—first working under supervision, receiving training, working "in the trenches" for years, and finally moving into counselor supervision and program direction. In my direct work with clients, I became convinced that we too often showed them their behaviors and even their motivations in a negative light, so I became committed to finding a positive approach. Later, I began to identify a need among the counselors I supervised for a therapeutic foundation in their work. So many of us are educated in a patchwork fashion that it seemed painfully obvious that we needed a unifying therapy.

My own patchwork looks something like this: First, I received training in Gestalt Therapy, coming to understand the internal conflict experienced by clients and the need for a spiritually-based integration to resolve it. Next, an educational background in Adlerian psychology taught me to regard all behavior as purposeful, and showed me the powerful tools that early memories can give us for identifying our perceptual base. Finally, training in Neuro-Linguistic Programming framed for me a clear, positive approach to treatment and offered specific tools for conducting therapy.

The result of applying my experience to addictions treatment is Perceptual Adjustment Therapy—the use of early client memories to identify positive intents and then using them to resolve a client's internal conflict.

Jim Holder
April, 1995

Chapter 1

FINDING THE SILVER LINING

Life is a mystery to be experienced rather than a problem to be solved.

Our present approach to addictions treatment in this country is essentially negative in its orientation. We encourage clients to stop dysfunctional behaviors and explore the means to stay stopped, but rarely consider what is to begin. We ask our clients to shun drinking and/or drugging, rather than identifying the purpose of that behavior and then finding positive, healthy ways of achieving the no drug/no drinking goal. We talk about relapse prevention, crisis avoidance, and guarding against numerous feelings, situations and people, or we talk about "white-knuckle" sobriety maintenance. We present a future of internal and external battles—a most unattractive prospect. Rarely do we talk about positively directing recovery, a going-toward rather than a running-from.

Perceptual Adjustment Therapy, or P.A.T., is grounded in the belief that all addicted clients are seeking some positive goal to achieve balance and wholeness, not just running from negative consequences. For example, an alcoholic might have had an early experience with alcohol that gave him/her an utterly wonderful feeling of calm, relaxation, and togetherness—a sense of well-being he/she would like to experience again and again. We all can understand and relate to this, yet counselors so seldom explore with clients the positive reasons underlying their use of the chemical. Instead, we focus on the client's need to stop using—the negative side of the issue.

To stop using is actually not a goal at all, assuming that a goal is something positive to be achieved. Continuing with our example, a goal that clients might choose may be to experience a feeling of peace and relaxation, whenever they desire, using their own resources. Helping clients identify positive goals is easy for clinicians once they fully understand the concept of *positive intents.*

Of course many counselors and therapists already are helping clients set positive goals for themselves; however, many of these clinicians do so inconsistently, which can cause confusion and imbalance among their clients. The focus of recovery is of vital importance: if we focus on the negative, we achieve the negative outcome; if we focus on the positive, the chances of obtaining the positive results are enhanced greatly.

Our goal in this book is twofold. First, we hope to assist clinicians in developing a simple, yet elegant treatment process that supports the client in achieving wholeness once again. This is accomplished by understanding the client's perceptions, which have caused voids in the client's life and set up a devastating internal conflict resulting in a choice between whether to use or not use chemicals. Second, we hope to give clinicians a better understanding of their own perceptions and how they influence the treatment process. A critical issue, in our view, is that those who counsel addicted clients maintain an ongoing process of therapy for themselves. The more often clinicians are in a balanced state, the more precise, focused, and successful they will be in their efforts.

With some clients who have lived in a depressed, negative state for years, in a society that focuses on not doing what's bad rather than doing what's good, and with the helper's natural human tendency to focus on the negativity of clients, the positive goals behind a client's behaviors may be difficult to find. Still, they are there if we look.

At ground level, one of the cornerstones for working with P.A.T. is that counselors must acquire and accept the idea that human behavior is purposeful and positively directed. No matter how bizarre or ridiculous a behavior may appear from the perspective of the observer or helper, there is a positive intent from the client's point of view. Identifying the positive intent is difficult only because it usually remains outside the client's conscious awareness.

Most counselors, when they are first introduced to a client and begin to establish some treatment goals, are sharp enough to put the burden of discovery on the client. That is, they begin by asking the client what they would like to get out of their treatment or what they hope to accomplish. The answer is most often in terms of what they want to learn *not to do* rather than learn what *to do.* They want to quit drinking; they want to stop spending all their money on cocaine; they want to stop going to jail; they want their families to stay off their backs. They will give us a "stop" negative rather than a "go" positive almost every time.

With P.A.T., we are going to learn to find the positive.

Consider this example of an alcoholic father of two boys. He had recently been arrested for D.U.I. while bringing his sons home from their Little League baseball game. The resultant fallout in the home and the social community had been pretty severe. As part of a plea bargain, the man's attorney had gotten the court to refer him to me for treatment. So when he comes in, what are the treatment goals he wants to set for himself? "I want to stop endangering the lives of my children." "I want to stop drinking." "I want to stay out of jail." "I want to stop ruining my reputation." And so on—all negative, or negative avoidance.

On the surface, these sound like valuable, workable treatment objectives. Beyond the obvious, however, remains the fact that his dysfunctional behaviors were all attempts to reach some positive goal. Without identifying this and finding functional ways to satisfy the intent, recovery is less than complete and lacks quality.

What might be some positive goals for this situation? One important approach involves asking the client what he/she will do when all has stopped that he/she wishes to stop. What will he/she do instead? If the client used to drink to relax, what can be done to accomplish that goal in a more functional way? The desire for relaxation is a very positive goal, one that can be essential for productivity at work and at home, for good health and personal satisfaction. For addicted people, the use and abuse of a chemical to achieve relaxation has become counterproductive and debilitating. The addict achieves just the opposite of the desired outcome—rather than relaxation, stress and dysfunction are created over the long run.

Let us look at the first goal in our example. The client said, "I want to stop endangering the lives of my children." To focus on endangering the children will only draw attention to the past for no good purpose. Instead of accepting his response, simply let the client know that he did not answer your question. Comfort the client, but point out that he let you know what he did *not* want rather than what he *did* want. Ask him directly, in positive terms, what are the goals he wants to set. In this particular example, the clinician might respond, "So what you do not want is to endanger your children—what is it that you do want?" The answer: "To keep them safe." Now that is a goal with which we can work.

His second statement was, "I want to stop drinking." To this I might respond, "If you focus on the fact that you don't want to drink, and your daily thoughts are on not drinking, and we restate this idea over and over again with our focus on not drinking or drinking, I'm afraid that's exactly what you'll accomplish—you'll drink."

Our minds have a peculiar way of deleting words and focusing only on the last idea or two. Think of a time when you said to someone (or they said to you) "I hope this or that doesn't happen," and then it immediately did. Probably we all have sat at a table and heard a parent say to a child, "Now, don't spill the milk," only to be followed by milk being spilled by someone.

That is what happens when we focus on not drinking—we achieve only what we are really trying to avoid. The last thing the brain hears and the action picture that it visualizes is what we *don't want* instead of what we are seeking. In this light, the objective "I want to stop drinking" is not helpful at all. Perhaps simply developing good physical health would be a better goal. The success of positive visualization in every arena from self-help to Olympic training is a quick testimony to this effect. The simplest way to arrive at our destinations is to discover our positive intents for going, then support them.

Returning to our example, what would be a more positive goal than "to stay out of jail"? Why not suggest something like, "I want to enjoy and appreciate my personal freedom." Similarly, we want to shift the emphasis from "I want to stop ruining my reputation" to "I want to build and enjoy a stable position in the community." Old-timers in A.A. are quick to point out that finding one simple idea to be grateful for can dispel almost any of the mind's immediate darkness and that keeping "first things first" is the foundation for lasting, contented sobriety.

To restate our client's goals, then, the father wanted

1. for his children to be safe,
2. to develop good physical health,
3. to enjoy his personal freedom, and
4. to build and enjoy a stable position in the community.

Worthwhile goals, wouldn't you say? As clinicians, the only barrier to our success with this method lies in reshaping our own preconceived ideas or, if you will, adjusting our perceptions.

To understand how useful this method can be, consider that when we use positive intents in setting the clients' goals, we have already begun the therapy.

That is, when you first challenge a client's perception of his/her role in life, new behavior will follow. Peter Laquere (1991) said, "First a person experiences new behavior, then there is awareness." Once it is put in an emotionally positive context, the client feels free to own the action and thereby take personal responsibility for his/her actions and life. We should stress that this is not an end in itself; rather, it is a beginning, a firm stepping stone for an ongoing journey.

To varying degrees, the fulfillment of positive intents is already being accomplished in most 12-step recovery programs. Two of the positive intents most often identified by clients are "to be sociable" and "to feel confident." Members of A.A. and its sister-fellowships go out of their way to make newcomers feel welcome and at ease. Group members tend to "bring along" new members as their own sobriety progresses, gaging their confidence and social comfort all the way. Typically, a newcomer might only be called on to make occasional comments at their first few meetings. Next, they might be asked to come early and greet people or help make coffee and feel more a part of the group. Soon the new member is sharing freely at discussion meetings and developing a network of A.A. friends with whom to socialize away from meetings. And after several months, the newcomer may be asked to tell his/her story at speaker meetings. It is remarkable, but in cities and towns around the world, you can regularly find an individual who only a year earlier needed to reach for a bottle to find the courage to drop in at a friend's Christmas party, standing by himself/ herself in front of a room filled with hundreds of people, sharing with them the very worst and the very best of his/her life experiences, turning what had been perceived as liabilities into assets.

We all have a desire to fit in or feel comfortable in society, and an awareness of our own needs helps us understand the needs of addicted clients. It is probably no accident that socially-related desires are the most frequently discovered positive intents for most addicts—people whose behaviors in the course of their worsening addictions are most often socially unacceptable. This sheds light, too, on the plight of those suffering from late-stage addiction and the nearly complete isolation it brings. In their delusional reality, they reach once again for the chemical that had once given them the courage to be outgoing.

You also can see why individual counseling techniques have gotten such a bad rap and have had such poor success in decades past. How could individual therapy work when the dependent person needs a social environment in which to develop new behavior patterns?

Today, professionals in the field are much more successful using group therapy, 12-step integration, group education classes, and the like. If clinicians will only fine-tune what they are saying (client goals) with what they are doing (group work), addictions medicine and therapy can take a quantum leap forward with higher recovery rates.

P.A.T. makes no attempt to avoid the obvious in approaching the addict's problem. Certainly a problem must be identified before a solution may be found. And yes, avoiding slippery places and not engaging in negative behaviors are important aspects of any addict's recovery. This is common sense from the perspective of the clinician. But in the client's interest, wouldn't it make more sense to reframe these ideas? Why not talk about spending time in safe places and engaging in positive behaviors? P.A.T. just uses a bit more *positive* common sense for an original, creative recovery process.

As with most initial assessments, we ask a client at what age he/she began using the chemical. This is useful for determining where the maturation process became altered, but it also helps us determine what positive intents underlay the early use. This is vitally important—the client's positive intents for early chemical use become clear, along with precise goals that have to be the focus of treatment for a *living recovery process* to occur. We call it a "living" recovery process because by overlooking the early positive intents, we in the field have unintentionally supported a death-like state: the *dry drunk*. Recovery should be an awakening of the total person physically, psychologically, and spiritually.

P.A.T. often begins by asking clients to recall their earliest childhood memory. To summarize the work of many *Adlerian* researchers, there is a proven relationship between our present ways of meeting life's problems and what is recalled from childhood. These childhood memories are a clear indication of our perceptions of life and our impressions of events. In fact, though early memories are among the most fascinating of clinical practices, their interpretation is simple to master.

Two primary reasons exist for using early memories in treating chemical dependency. First, it allows us to understand how an individual drinks or uses drugs. Second, it is the first available indicator of a person's positive intents for use.

Please note that *how* an individual uses is very different from *why* an individual uses. A.A. old-timers are quick to remind us that why isn't the issue; similarly, Gestalt Therapy, which heavily influences P.A.T., agrees. Fritz Perls, the developer of *Gestalt Therapy*, used to say, "*Why* is a mind game; *how* is what's important." And we agree. In addition, P.A.T. looks at the larger picture of how a person uses—that is, the way in which a person deludes themselves into using. For example, a person who is scared to dance might say, "Well, I'll have a few beers to give myself a little confidence." He drinks, feels more confident, and asks a woman to dance. After a few moments his fear may return, so he has another drink to bring his confidence back to a suitable level. This cycle continues all evening and is a primary focus for P.A.T.

Another example of the "how" process can be drawn from watching people learn to swim. The process of swimming, especially for children, is much more than being in the water and stroking. It includes getting dressed or undressed, putting on lotion or sunscreen, getting in a car to travel, having money to pay if necessary, and, as a Cherokee healer once said of the fantasy of the shared experience, having "The wonderful thought of being joyful with friends." These are all part of our how picture, along with our relationship to the water. What is meant by relationship is how the water reacts to us and how we react to the water. The *how* encompasses the totality of the experience.

Over a seven-year period at a hospital-based addictions treatment unit, we collected a strong though informal sampling of early memories from alcohol and drug addicted clients. Out of 50 addicted clients who were asked their first memory, 84% of either the events occurring or the feelings associated with first memories were negative. Of these, almost one-half were fear-based.

This means that most of the people in treatment believe that people in general (men, women, or authority figures) or in many cases life itself is scary. No wonder trust issues are so essential with addicted people. If life is perceived as threatening, people will protect themselves.

Imagine going through life with fear being one of your most frequently experienced feelings. If, for example, you have developed a perceptual filter that social situations are scary, then even when a social situation is fun—perhaps when you should be having the best time you have had in years—there is an undercurrent of fear reaching in, a sense that something painful is going to happen. Then imagine that after enduring this torment for a long time, you have your first few drinks of alcohol. Lo and behold, feelings of warmth, comfort, and confidence immediately dispel the fear you have felt almost constantly for years. What a wonderful experience! Now ask yourself, what would my relationship be to alcohol? Would I drink again? Of course. Most people would.

Some have argued that these feelings of comfort and confidence are illusions perceived by the addict. P.A.T. approach is exactly the opposite. We believe that our perceptions and feelings are among the most "real" of our life experiences; in fact, our reality is altered to accommodate our perceptions of reality. In the process of addiction, the only illusion is that acquiring the feelings of comfort and confidence in this manner is harmless. Giving up personal responsibility to a substance or anything else can be devastating in its consequences.

Significant with regard to our findings with early childhood memories is the remarkable consistency our findings share with a well-documented body of research conducted by Adlerian psychologists.

Our sampling looks at the outstanding characteristics of first memories and takes from them essential thematic information that can predict or confirm certain ideas about the addict's present situation. The more memories we gather, the clearer the belief systems become. Inconsistencies can alert a therapist to look for other information or events.

For example, many cocaine addicts have first memories that are related to excitement or being "up," often interrupted or concluded with some sort of negative event—an accident, being punished, etc. . . . Now, were a cocaine addict's first memory to be completely inconsistent with this—a warm, gentle memory of well-being, for instance—the therapist would be alerted to look for a death in the family, abuse, or other life trauma.

More than just a check-sheet, though, first memories and the ensuing interviews can give the therapist even better information with regard to the positive intents underlying the addict's chemical use. We first developed these techniques from *Neuro-Linguistic Programmers*, who suggested that teaching clients to satisfy their original positive intents may be among the most effective means to treat individuals and families.

And finally, P.A.T. focuses on the internal conflict that occurs within the person. No matter what the presenting problem is, no matter what the client says the problem is, whenever someone walks into a therapist's office seeking help, he/she is in conflict somehow. Within all of our clients are at least two powerful factions at war with each other. If there was not a split, they would be "together," and they would not need us.

P.A.T. has been influenced heavily by Gestalt Therapy and, specifically, its originator Fritz Perls. In the late sixties, Perls was addressing these polarities within clients. He dealt with them differently from other therapists in that he saw polarities as representing conflict and a constant process in life. As soon as one set of polarities was integrated, another was uncovered, much like layers of an onion. A woman may be getting dressed and want to put on a bright red dress that flatters her figure. Then she thinks, "But I shouldn't wear something provocative to work." The battle has been joined, and however it is resolved, when that resolution occurs, a new set of polarities will emerge to face the individual.

The most renowned of these polarities Perls called the "top dog" and "underdog" split. It is really very simple. The *top dog* is very authoritative, very parent-like. The top dog tells you how you should live, how you ought to be. We all have a part of ourselves that is like that, the part that really gets down on us. Its positive aspects are that it gives us some boundaries and sets up personal guidelines. The *underdog* is a manipulative game-player, usually disguised in sly roles we play with emotionalism, defensiveness, and apologies. Use of the underdog can even be covertly rebellious, saying, "Sure, I'll do what you want," and then doing the opposite or nothing at all. Some positive aspects of the underdog lie in its childlike quality: it is more fun-loving and can be more spontaneous. So there are positives and negatives to both polarities. The cunning and cleverness of the underdog usually enable it to "win" most of its encounters though it would appear to have no power at all—one of life's great paradoxes.

The top dog/underdog game is only one of many tormenting polarity games individuals may play with themselves. Spin-offs may include passive/aggressive, helpless/angry, and in this book we will focus on an *abstaining/chemical using split*.

Dependent people basically have a full range of polarities like many other people; however, the first one we must deal with in treatment is that of abstaining/chemical using. The conflict to use or not use rages in the dependent client, and although it appears to resemble the top dog/underdog split and shares many of that classic conflict's characteristics, we won't call it that and will address it separately because of unique forms it takes owing to the dependency.

The dependent person's conflict has an additional phenomenon, that is, an alternative personality that takes shape with the use of the chemical. We might call it the *chemical person*. This alternative personality gives the individual the delusion that he/she has filled the holes or voids created by his/her normal personal roles in life. An example might be the quiet, reserved individual who has thrown away his/her courageous self and even forgotten it ever existed. The person never forgets wanting it, and under the influence of the chemical, the individual feels, acts, and sounds courageous.

Keep in mind that we are not talking about multiple personality disorder. People with that condition usually are not aware of the division within themselves; clients with abstaining/using conflicts are keenly aware of the split. They will talk to you about it, and about the feelings they associate with each, the internal dialogue they maintain, and the fear, guilt, and resentment that permeate their lives.

With alcohol and drug clients, the split is far apart or distinct. One part is out and is what you see. The other part is withdrawn and sort of quiet. Logically, the abstaining side is the part of the addict that wants to stay clean, and the using side is the part that wants to accomplish a positive intent by using a chemical. The rift between these sides and the characteristics they maintain are predictable and very reliable clinically.

It should be noted that the using side is present without the chemical itself being there. Many times a family member might tell a client, "You're getting ready to go get drunk. I know it." They are right more often than not, because they have seen the personality switch take place. Once the decision has been made to get drunk, the person looks different, sounds different, and feels different; then the behavior changes. The using side "wins" completely and steps up on stage.

At this point in our look at the split within an addicted client, it is important to make note of one essential fact: each half hates the other. The abstaining side is scared of the using side, and resents it for the loss, the fear, and the embarrassing situations it creates. In many cases, the using side resents the abstaining side's attitude, the fact that the abstaining side never has any fun, is always scared (the dry drunk), and covers it up by being self-righteous and dogmatic.

To address this, P.A.T. encourages the dependent person to accept the positive aspects of both sides. Through the search for positive intents, the dependent person can accept responsibility for the actions of each. This newfound acceptance and responsibility is the beginning of the integrative processes that bring wholeness and a sense of oneness with one's self and a higher power. To become responsible for finding healthy, chemical free ways of achieving these positive intents is to become whole, a unique spiritual being.

BIBLIOGRAPHY

Colker, A., & Slaymaker, B. (1984). Early recollections of alcoholics. *Individual Psychology, 1,* 30–38.

Hafner, J.L., Fakouri, M.E., & Labrentz, H.L. (1982). First memories of "normal" and alcoholic individuals. *Individual Psychology, 3,* 238–244.

Laquere, P. (1991). In film presentation by Paul Thorington, First Annual Conference on Multiple Family Therapy, Florence, SC.

Chapter **2**

DESTINED FOR ADDICTION

There are no "chance memories"; out of the incalculable number of impressions which meet an individual, he chooses to remember only those which he feels, however darkly, to have a bearing on his situation.

Alfred Adler

When we ask a client for a first memory, the report we get does not just "happen" to be recalled. It is the exact memory, culled from all the rest, that the client's own mind interprets as somehow reflecting his present situation. It is like asking a child to draw a picture of his family and then inferring from it some clues about their relationships, or better, about the child's perception of their relationships.

In all likelihood, a client's first memory did not cause his or her addiction. This is vital to understanding P.A.T.: we are not looking for an explicit cause for a client's addiction. Instead, we're looking for a way to understand a client's perceptions, and early memories give us a road map to his/her perceptions. As for tracking down the cause of an addiction, we hold that it is the combined result of many inputs (among the oldest theories in the field). However, P.A.T. does assert the following regarding addiction's cause: persistent negative feelings, such as pain and fear, set up an intense longing for the positive feelings that accompany positive life experiences, which may be temporarily and artificially invoked through chemicals.

In the words of thousands of addicted people: "I wanted to feel normal."

Addiction is accomplished only through the repetitive use of a chemical, to the point at which the body is altered and believes "normal" is under the chemical's influence. Of course, psychological dependence can be established far more rapidly than physical addiction, and many recovering people report a psychological dependency that began with the experimental phase of their chemical use.

In the quote from Adler that opened this chapter, the words "however darkly" stand out ominously. In our sample, 84% of the memories we acquired from addicted clients were negative in their orientation, and we maintain that the early memories of addicts are primarily those of pain and fear. By opening ourselves to the use of those memories and their "dark" qualities, we avail ourselves of a vital link to the client's perceptions, the client's addiction and thus, the client's treatment.

In this chapter, we will examine the relationship between early memories and addiction. This will show how to use early memories to assess the positive intents, guiding fictions, and perceptual filters underlying an addict's chemical use. Next, in specific case examples, we will look at ways to help clients use their own early memories to become aware of their life's patterns on both emotional and intellectual levels.

Our patterns for living are established early, some say by the time we are six years old. Afterwards, we tend to process our experiences through that which we learned in those early years. That is, we make sense of things and incorporate events into our individual makeup in unique ways. Adler called this our *private logic,* and the terms of that logic are largely established powerfully and quickly. There is a lot to learn in our early years, and we seem to learn well. This doesn't mean that we learn objectively or even accurately; rather, what we do learn becomes very deeply ingrained.

In treatment, when portions of clients' lives have become dysfunctional, accessing these early lessons gives clients objective awareness of their perceptions and the opportunity to challenge the accuracy of the lessons. Our perception of events determines our attitudes and behaviors, so if the perceptions are limited, our options for action become limited as well. These perceptions set up filters through which clients interpret daily events, and it is by seeing those filters for what they are that clients will begin to change them.

We all use these filters to one degree or another; some of us perceive the world's events as being dangerous to us personally, others of us may see the world through rose-colored glasses. But with the addict, the process has another loop. The filtering process distorts actual events, changing them to jive with a limiting perception, and denial begins. This happens early, usually years before any chemical use, and once chemicals are introduced, a whole pattern of delusional thinking develops. By becoming aware of this process and making necessary options available in response to their own frustration and pain, clients can assume personal responsibility for their whole lives and become balanced once again.

Figure 2.1. is an illustration of how the perceptual filter operates. We observe an event taking place, and with the intellect of a child, we interpret the experience. The decision we make sets up a perceptual filter that we use to guide us through our world. An infant experiences short and tall people, honest and dishonest people, and so on. A child between the ages of one and seven may have an experience that the child chooses to see in a specific manner and generalizes this perception to all experience. For example, the perception this child chooses is that all people are dishonest. The perceptual filter is in place, and honest people no longer exist in that child's world.

The process of change is a paradoxical one, much as Fritz Perls believed. Change occurs the moment a person accepts himself/herself as he/she is. At that moment, the internal conflict is resolved, and the person becomes balanced. To say it another way, trying to be different or change is futile, but to accept who you are with all your qualities is change in itself and is wonderfully rewarding.

Major personality changes require a catalyst. Some traumatic event or disaster, therapy, or a spiritual experience, but not much else, can make it happen. The motive forces behind our lives are too well entrenched. Among these motive forces are what Adler called *fictive notions* or **guiding fictions**—ideas that may not be entirely true but which our behavior would suggest we regard as absolute truth. Examples of these guiding fictions among addicted clients may

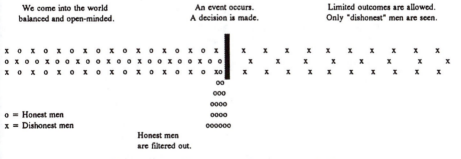

Figure 2.1.   Illustration of a perceptual filter.

include such ideas as "people can't be trusted," "life is dangerous," or maybe "I am worthless." Because these ideas inform our choice-making structures as adults, *P.A.T. uses guiding fictions as a focal point in treatment.*

Adler coined the term *lifestyle* and defined it as, essentially, your response to the sum of your guiding fictions and perceptions, the style or role you pick for living. Erick Burns, the father of Transactional Analysis, called it your *life script*. Perls referred to it as the role you choose or your character. Once persons pick a personality, character, lifestyle, life script or role in life, they must set aside parts of themselves they deem to be in conflict with their daily situations and soon forget these parts ever existed. This denial of one's self is where so many of us get into trouble.

In Figure 2.2 to begin with, balance exists between shyness and outgoingness. Then an event happens and a perception is made: "Life is dangerous." The perception is followed by a decision: "Since life is dangerous, I must protect myself by being reserved, cautious, and quiet." The role of being shy is chosen, and the perceptual filter is developed. The individual then goes on to deny his/her outgoing self.

Soon, the family jumps in and supports the role, strengthening the perceptual filter and its implicit denial. For example, one of her mother's friends asks young Susie how old she is. Susie turns and puts her face in her mother's skirt. Mom replies, "Oh! Susie's so shy!" At this point, Mom and Susie are both in denial.

In Figure 2.3 it is illustrated how a filter is blocked by use of chemicals. When a chemical is used, the filter vanishes. The outgoing self is released from exile, and the person feels talkative and sociable. Believing this chemical made him/her outgoing, he/she once again denies the outgoing self by giving the chemical the responsibility for his/her actions.

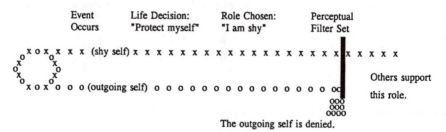

Figure 2.2. Illustration of how a perceptual filter is developed.

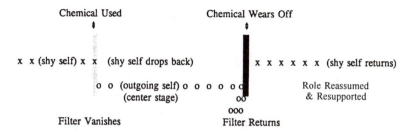

Figure 2.3. Illustration of use of chemical to block the filter.

Once the chemical has worn off, the perceptual filter is back in place, and once again the person takes on the shy role and denies the outgoing self.

Whether or not our guiding fictions are true or accurate does not matter. What stands out instead is that those guiding fictions are our own creations, and we have the power to alter our own creations. *P.A.T. may be understood best as a way of showing clients this simple fact and supporting them in their choices and assumption of personal responsibility.*

HERE AND NOW

Just as they may or may not be totally true, our earliest memories may or may not even have happened. And from a therapeutic standpoint, the difference is unimportant. *What is important is the metaphor, the map of the way people perceive life to be and the route they plan to take.* Some of the early memories "recalled" are dreams or daydreams. In many cases, clients do not have a complete conscious memory of an event that occurred in early childhood, not the way they remember yesterday's supper. They have a few fragments (images, colors, feelings); they have some conscious information (for example, where they were living at the time, what people might have been present, etc.), and that is about it.

A lack of information can be telling. Whatever the client gives you will be part of the role or character they are playing out, part of the perceptual field that you and the client are discovering. Remember, there is no bad information, only different maps. Filling in the holes between pieces so perfectly that the subjects themselves cannot tell the difference is done by the subconscious mind. So, either our subconscious affects the choice of an existing accurate memory or dream, or it "fills in the blanks" in our earliest childhood images. Regardless, the resulting report is one of the most accurate maps we may have to a client's subconscious mind. And what does this map show us? The guiding fictions behind a person's lifestyle.

Sometimes we can be amazed at how simple this seems. From ages one to seven, we make decisions about how we will perceive life. We grasp these decisions as if they were real, and then live out our lives as young adults and adults based on decisions we made as children. Now, if you ask a person to live his/her life the way a four-year-old tells them to, he/she probably would say you are nuts. But the fact is, most people are already living out their lives in this very manner.

Although we use early memories, P.A.T. remains firmly rooted in the here and now. We truly believe that dealing in the here and now is the only way to restore ourselves to balance. The past has no real importance to us in our present problems. When you ask for a general early memory, it gives clients freedom to go to a memory with emotional relevance to their present situation and the way they live today. The early memories they choose will become a subconscious metaphor on their part to show you the world as they perceive it here and now. This gives you, the clinician, an elegant way of seeing their current perceptions, their guiding fictions for life as they now live it, and the gaps left in their perceptual field. Furthermore, when clients have feelings about an event, past or present, that brings the event into the here and now.

Perhaps your employer requires you to ask certain questions of all your clients during an initial visit—"Were you ever sexually abused," "Were you ever physically abused," or "Did your father ever strike your mother"—specific questions that may or may not have emotional relevance to the client in the here and now. This directs the client into the past, leaving his/her present world of experience behind. This weakens the quality of information you can receive and dilutes the treatment process. Routine sets of questions force both the clinician and the client into the client's past, and the clinician is left with the responsibility of interpreting events through his/her own perceptual field and deciding what is best for the client. The result is often a treatment plan that would benefit the counselor more than the client.

THEMATIC INFORMATION FROM MEMORIES

To understand how early childhood memories offer us thematic information, consider the following scenario (which actually took place) in which one client, a cocaine addict, was sharing an early memory with his therapist in the presence of other clients, one of whom was alcoholic:

COCAINE ADDICT: *I was about four years old and was riding a tricycle. Fast. I was flying down this hill in front of our house. I remember the wind blowing in my face. Then I crossed the street into our neighbor's yard. Then I rammed into a tree.*

THERAPIST: *What's the feeling you associate with the memory?*

ALCOHOLIC: (Interrupting) *Pain, man, pain!*

THERAPIST: (To the cocaine addict) *Really? What's the feeling you associate with it?*

COCAINE ADDICT: *Excitement! Thrill! Flying! It was great!*

THERAPIST: (To the alcoholic) *Watch the difference between your perceptions.*

THERAPIST: (To the cocaine addict) *Which part of the memory stands out to you?*

ALCOHOLIC: (Interrupting again) *Hitting the tree!*

COCAINE ADDICT: (Asserting himself) *No—the wind blowing through my hair while I rode as fast as I could.*

THERAPIST: (To the alcoholic) *Is your drug of choice alcohol?*

ALCOHOLIC: (Puzzled) *Yes.*

THERAPIST: (To the cocaine addict) *Is your drug of choice cocaine?*

COCAINE ADDICT: *Yes.*

THERAPIST: *Cocaine addicts are often excitement seekers and actually get two highs from their drug—the excitement from doing something dangerous or illegal, and the high from the cocaine. Alcoholics are more often fear-based, and are usually seeking a release or a better feeling.*

THERAPIST: (To the alcoholic) *Does your first memory involve pain?*

ALCOHOLIC: *Yes.*

THERAPIST: (To the group) *We need to remember that when we ask a question or make an assumption, it usually comes from our perceptions. That's OK, as long as we own those perceptions as our own and accept that they may not fit the person telling the memory.*

Clearly, the two clients perceived this event differently. P.A.T. holds that this perceptual difference is not chance; nor is it affected in any significant way by the interjection of different drugs themselves. Rather, these clients' positive intents for using were related directly to their drugs of choice. In fact, there can be numerous positive intents and just as many drugs that the client feels satisfy those various positive intents. We are also fully aware that once an individual becomes physically addicted, they will often use any drug they can get their hands on, especially in a crisis. This will be discussed further in Chapter 3.

CASE EXAMPLES

In the examples of actual memories that follow, we will follow this outline:

1. The memory itself, word for word as the client reported it.
2. The therapist asking the client what was the most significant part of the memory and the feeling the client associates with it.
3. In some cases, a specific question from the therapist that was prompted by some statement(s) from the client.
4. The giving to clients of more responsibility for the memory by asking questions.
5. The unfolding of the session so that what you will see are the client's statements the way the therapist saw them, the questions those statements prompted, and the client's answers to those questions.
6. Since these memories were obtained in the context of an edu-therapy group, how these memories allowed the clients themselves to see the relationship between early memories and positive intents, along with the chemical use that followed.
7. How clients could clearly see and own their responsibility for the chemical use and addiction by coming to understand the gaps left in their perceptual field—the behavioral, emotional, and spiritual voids they sought to fill with chemicals.
8. When conducting the group, this understanding was the sole objective.

When a client grasped and accepted this idea, the therapist would move on to another client. In ongoing work with the client, the therapist would continue to look for guiding fictions and the perceptual gaps they caused; therefore, the "Additional Questions" are presented to assist you in conducting a more thorough assessment of the client's situation.

9. The last section of each example centers upon positive intents—again, a verbatim exchange with the client. These translate into specific goals for treatment. This will be valuable later as P.A.T. takes a more in-depth look at goal-setting.

Finally, an admonition before beginning with case: *Abandon now any ideas you may have about finding* causes *for addiction.* These memories will not show us causes, and that is not what we are looking for. These memories show us the client's *perceptions* with regard to *how* they use chemicals, and that is material we can work with.

Example 1

Client: White male
Age: Early 30s
Addiction: Alcohol

"I was about 3, coming up on my third Christmas. I was with my three brothers, and my aunt was with us. My mother and father went out shopping. We let the neighbor's cat in, and it ran under the Christmas tree. We ran to get the cat before Mom and Dad would catch us. I was standing as my brother went under the tree and caused it to tilt. I was pushing on it, trying to hold it up, and the tree fell on me while we were trying to get the cat out. Bulbs were breaking on the floor as the tree was falling over. And the door opened. I was under the tree and last to run. I was racing my brothers to the bedroom and I fell in the hallway. I was the first one my father grabbed. We got our butts cut and sent to bed early without seeing Santa. We still got presents that night, even though the last thing I heard my mother saying was 'Nothing but stockings full of coal in this house tonight.' But we got presents."

Most memorable aspect: The tree falling simultaneously as the front door opened.

Feeling(s) associated: "Being scared to death."

THERAPIST: *Do you have a belief that when you do something wrong, you'll get in trouble?*

CLIENT: *When I do something wrong, I'm going to get caught.*

("I was pushing on it, trying to hold it up, and the tree fell on me while we were trying to get the cat out.")

THERAPIST: *Is there a pattern of getting in trouble when you try to help out?*

CLIENT: *No matter how hard I try to help others, things just fall apart.*

(" 'Nothing but stockings full of coal in this house tonight.' But we got presents.")

THERAPIST: *Do you have a hard time trusting people?*

CLIENT: *I hold back at first.*

THERAPIST: *Do you feel like consequences will never be as bad as people threaten?*

CLIENT: *People usually give me what I want.*

THERAPIST: *What is Christmas like for you today?*

CLIENT: *Very emotional.*

Note: Occupations are quite often related to the memory. (Most memorable aspect: The tree falling simultaneously as the front door opened.)

THERAPIST: *What do you do for a living?*

CLIENT: *I cut trees for power lines.*

GROUP: (Laughter)

CLIENT: *Oh, and by the way, I can't stand cats.*

GROUP: (Much laughter)

Note: The client is now relating his perceptions to the memory on his own, which makes it easier for him to take responsibility for his behaviors.

THERAPIST: *Do you feel that the scare is in getting caught, not in the actual consequence?*

CLIENT: *The fear is in not pleasing my family.*

Additional Questions:

"Does the number three hold great importance for you?" (It came up three times in the first part of the memory.)
"Do you believe that women won't carry through with what they say?"

Determining Positive Intents for Using Chemicals:

THERAPIST: *What do you think are your positive goals for using?*

CLIENT: *To fit in with other guys.*

THERAPIST: *To be sociable?*

CLIENT: *Yes.*

THERAPIST: *Any others?*

CLIENT: *To relax. I guess I used alcohol for approval and to feel more courageous. And I used to feel accepted by people.*

Note: "To be accepted" and "to fit in with other guys" are very similar; when the client begins repeating himself/herself with positive intents, that is a good time to stop.

THERAPIST: *Do you find social situations a little scary, like in the memory?*

CLIENT: *Yes.*

THERAPIST: *And the fear disappears when you're high?*

CLIENT: *Yes.*

THERAPIST: *You become relaxed, feel more sociable, have courage and feel accepted by others?*

CLIENT: *Yes.*

THERAPIST: (To the group) *Aren't these positive intents something we'd all like? To fit in, be approved of, be accepted, and be coura- geous—without the use of chemicals?*

GROUP: *Yes.*

Note: Consider giving the client homework. You might ask him to try to identify the anxious feeling that he associates with the mem- ory, and to notice when it starts to pop up in his daily life. For instance, it might come along when he is playing volleyball with the group or having fun somehow. If, when he notices it, he will ask the group to reassure him that everything is okay, and he will reassure himself that everything is okay, his guiding fiction will have been confronted and begun to change. Oh, and by the way, I would ask him to make sure, as he is having fun, that what he is doing is within the rules.

Example 2

Client: White Male
Age: Late 30s
Addiction: Alcohol

"I don't know, I may have been 3 or 4. I remember playing outside in the dirt with my brother who was using cusswords. He told me to say them. I did. My father came tearing around the corner of the house. He had been under the car, where he always was. He was mad and was fussing at us. We were all taken in the house, and I don't know what he did to them. He washed my mouth out with soap, and it was a long time before I could wash my mouth out or have a drink."

Most memorable aspect: His dad being mad.

Feeling(s) associated: "Confusion."

THERAPIST: *Do you look for approval from others?*

CLIENT: *Yes. I look for other people to say I'm doing a good job.*

("He told me to say them. I did. . . . He washed my mouth out with soap.")

THERAPIST: *Do you have any feelings around when to express yourself?*

CLIENT: *I'm afraid to let mine out. My feelings out.*

THERAPIST: *Do you always do what others tell you to do?*

CLIENT: *I've been very dependent all my life.*

Additional Questions:

"What's your occupation?" (It would be interesting to see if he works with dirt or automobiles.)
"Do you feel like authority figures stay under things, hide, or sneak around?"
"Do you find that things happen to you when you least expect them?"

Determining Positive Intents for Using Chemicals:

THERAPIST: *What do you think are your positive goals for using?*

CLIENT: *To feel good. To dance. To talk to strangers.*

THERAPIST: *Your positive intents are all in the memory: feeling good, when you're afraid to let your feelings out; to talk, when talking gets you in trouble; and dancing is an adult form of play or expressing feelings, both of which get you in trouble.*

Perceptual Filters: The client has given up his own sense of self-approval—"Others have to tell me when I'm doing good." The client has given up his social self—talking and expressing his feelings get him into trouble.

Note: When clients have drinking or some form of drinking in their early memories, alcohol is often their drug of choice. To avoid making assumptions, be sure to ask the client a question that will give you an answer.

Now that you have seen a couple of these early memories and their relationship to the clients' present situations, you can probably begin to understand the importance of positive intents to clients and the conflict we set up when we ask them to stop using the chemicals without finding new ways to satisfy their positive intents.

Example 3

> Client: White Female
> Age: Mid-40s
> Addiction: Alcohol/Diet Pills

"I was about 3 years old, and my dad managed a place in town. I had a parakeet. I was told never to turn the fan on without first putting our bird in the cage. I put the bird in the cage, and I thought the door was shut. But the door came open and the bird flew out into the fan and was hurt. I kept watching for Dad to come home. When Dad drove up, I ran out, and Dad ran up the steps. He thought something was wrong with my brother. He was relieved when he found out that only the bird was hurt. We put whiskey and water on the bird's leg, and he got better."

Most memorable aspect: Watching for dad to come home, seeing dad running up the stairs.

Feeling(s) associated: "Guilt."

("We put whiskey and water on the bird's leg, and he got better.")

THERAPIST: *How do you use alcohol in your life today?*

CLIENT: *I use alcohol when I hurt.*

("I put the bird in the cage, and I thought the door was shut.")

THERAPIST: *Do you have a feeling, even when you do something carefully, that something may go wrong?*

CLIENT: *No matter how hard I try, it's not enough.*

Note: This client's fear of something going wrong had caused deep problems for her, to the point that she would wake up at night afraid that everything in the house wasn't turned off or secured.

("I had a parakeet.")

THERAPIST: *Do you still enjoy animals?*

CLIENT: *I have a compassion for animals.*

("My dad managed a place in town. . . . I kept watching for Dad to come home. . . . He thought something was wrong with my brother.")

THERAPIST: *Are you still close to your dad?*

CLIENT: *Dad is still real important to me.*

THERAPIST: *I notice there are only males mentioned in the memory.*

CLIENT: *Mom had fussed at me; Bob was in the hospital.*

Additional Questions:

"Do you feel men are helpful and that women fuss?"
"Do you have a pattern of stopping and waiting for help when you have a problem?"
"Do you feel that men can take care of problems best?"
"Do you feel insignificant?"

Determining Positive Intents for Using Chemicals:
Alcohol: "In the evening, to feel good and relax."
Amphetamines (Diet Pills): "To have more energy and work around the house—fluff pillows and things."

Here was a young lady who decided to do a menial task around the house (turn the fan on). There was a problem; she made a mistake.

Now she has a belief or filter that she can't do things. She set the "action" part of herself aside. Now she takes amphetamines in order to initiate action and let that part of herself out. This client may believe that a woman's primary place in life is her home; further, when she's there, she has an underlying fear that she will forget something and when she does forget something, there is a pronounced feeling of guilt. Therefore, she drinks alcohol to feel good and relax.

Example 4

>Client: White Female
>Age: Mid-50s
>Addiction: Xanax

>*"I was about 4 years old, and I remember waking up hearing my mom scream. My dad was beating her up. She said: 'Leave me alone,' and 'Don't wake up the baby.' I was in bed by myself and I just laid there, scared. I had trouble sleeping. I thought it was all my fault."*

Most memorable aspect: "Mamma screaming."

Feeling(s) associated: "Being scared."

>*("I remember waking up hearing my mom scream. . . . I had trouble sleeping.")*

>**THERAPIST:** *Do you have any trouble sleeping?*

>**CLIENT:** *Yes. I can't stand to be alone. I sleep during the day with my husband.*

>*("My dad was beating her up.")*

>**THERAPIST:** *Do you fight with your husband?*

>**CLIENT:** *I start fighting when he does. And I say to myself that men are all that way.*

>*("I thought it was all my fault.")*

>**THERAPIST:** *One important part of this memory is that you assumed responsibility for the event and felt guilty. Do you have strong feelings that when something goes wrong, it's your fault?*

>**CLIENT:** *Yes.*

Additional Questions:

"Do you tend to freeze up during a crisis?"
"Do you feel life is scary or that people are scary?"

"Do you feel like women get their power through screaming?" or
"Do you feel women are noisy but have very little power?"

Determining Positive Intents for Using Chemicals:

THERAPIST: *What are your positive reasons for using chemicals?*

CLIENT: *Feeling calm* (as opposed to scared). *To fit in with the crowd* (instead of being alone). *To express my feelings, to talk* (as opposed to lying there, scared).

This client's positive intents make a lot of sense in light of the memory. She said, "I can't stand being alone," yet she is scared to take action with others. That is a terrible conflict. So early on she made a decision to protect herself and remain quiet. So the talkative, social side of her personality was buried and only came out when she used the chemical. She began to "fit in" when she was high instead of feeling alone, and to top it all off, a feeling of calm came over her when she was high that replaced her fear.

Her denial is easy to understand. Would you want to admit you are addicted when you thought it meant giving up the accomplishment of all these positive intents?

Note that these first four examples are generally typical of alcoholics and addicts who choose depressant drugs or a combination of alcohol and other drugs. They are negative in the feelings associated with the memory or the events themselves. Either way, it is easy to see how the memories are related to the positive intents underlying the later chemical use.

Also note that while these tendencies are useful clinical guidelines, we can not take them for granted. If we do, we'll find ourselves directing clients away from truly individualized treatment goals.

There are not a lot of adults who are only marijuana users. However, Example 5 shows an early memory that fits the overall pattern of negativity among addicts' early memories. This negativity is related directly to the client's chemical use, both emotionally and materially.

Example 5

Client: White Male
Age: Late 40s
Addiction: Marijuana

"I was 5 or 6 years old. I had gotten my first go-cart for Christmas. I was driving circles around the house. I'd go around and around. There was a little girl who wanted to ride my go-cart, and she stood in front of me. I asked her 3 times to get out of my way, or I would run over her. She didn't move. So I ran over her. I remember looking down and she was looking up at me hollerin'. I lost my go-cart that day."

Most memorable aspect: "The little girl hollerin'."

Feeling(s) associated: Fear.

("I asked her 3 times to get out of my way, or I would run over her. She didn't move. So I ran over her.")

THERAPIST: *Are you a person who likes to have your own way?*

CLIENT: *I love having my own way* (big smile).

("I'd go around and around.")

THERAPIST: *Do you find you go in circles at times?*

CLIENT: *Yes. There are times I end up right back where I started.*

(The client described his first use as feeling like he was "walking on clouds.")

THERAPIST: *The nice things about clouds is that nothing gets in your way.*

Determining Positive Intents for Using Chemicals:

THERAPIST: *So what do you think were your positive reasons for using chemicals?*

CLIENT: *To have something that people wanted.* (This client was a drug dealer. He was used to having something that people wanted. The little girl wanted the go-cart.)

CLIENT: *Being sociable.* (He is a person who probably has a hard time with relationships [especially with women] since he likes so much to have his own way.)

CLIENT: *Being carefree.* (This is likely a perception that, "When I'm having fun, someone will try to mess it up"—an underlying feeling of fear.)

Additional Questions:

"Do you feel that when you're having fun, someone will get in your way?"
"Do you have an underlying feeling of fear?"
"What's your occupation?"

The next two examples are memories of cocaine addicts and follow the general theme of other addicts' memories in their negative orientation. However, note the theme of excitement in these memories. In one, it is overt and expressed; in the other, it is present in an underlying quality of hustle and bustle. Many times, cocaine addicts will be fear-based like an alcoholic, the cocaine giving them courage and initiative to act.

Example 6

Client: Black Female
Age: Early 30s
Addiction: Alcohol/Cocaine

"I was in kindergarten, Mrs. Jones' class. It was sleep-time, and everybody was supposed to be asleep. Another little boy and I got under the table and were coloring in our crayon books. The table sat by the door, and I always played at it. It had a tea set, puzzles and big blocks."

Most memorable aspect: The little boy and I being under the table.

Feelings associated: Devilish. Conniving.

Several people in the group smiled or laughed, suggesting there may have been a sexual component to the event. She said defensively, "Now wait a minute, there was nothing sexual about it."

I asked her if there were ways she was devilish and conniving now. She said yes, she was sneaky now. I'm devilish and sneaky with men. This is consistent with the way she tried to hide the sexual overtones of this first memory and is borne out by the following, her second memory, which she recalled soon after.

"My second memory is also from kindergarten. We were behind a tree at Mrs. Jones' school. A fat boy fondled me. I kept running around and around the tree and he kept chasing me."

Most memorable aspect: He was a fat boy.

Feeling(s) associated: "I was mad."

At first she was sneaky but, with some awareness, she took responsibility and shared the second memory with the group. This is a good sign for the therapist, an indicator that treatment is starting to work, for this is the same process clients must undergo to take ownership of who they are.

Determining Positive Intents for Using Chemicals:

THERAPIST: *What were your positive reasons for using chemicals?*

CLIENT: (RE: Stealing alcohol from her father) *To feel grown up.* (Note the "sneaky" parallel.)

CLIENT: (RE: Pot) *To be more sexual.*

CLIENT: (RE: Cocaine) *For a rush, to feel "hyped up."* (Perhaps cocaine has two "rushes" for her—doing something illegal or sneaky, and the physical rush the chemical produces.)

Additional Questions:

"Do you stay in situations even when you're getting nowhere?"
"Do you get motivated to move when you're mad?"
"When you're mad, do you feel like you run in circles?"
"Do you realize that there are no consequences in your memory?"
"Are you obvious when you're being sneaky—like being under the table but in plain sight?"
"Would there be some ways that you're not up front with men?"
"Do you have the feeling you want to run in sexual situations?"

Example 7

Client: White Male
Age: Late 20s
Addiction: Cocaine

"I remember when I was 2. Me and my aunt and Mother took my father to a big boat. We all hugged and kissed and he got on the boat. And at the time the ship pulled off, I remember seeing my father on top of the ship. And I remember coming home without him. Later on that night, I remember taking my mom into the hospital, and she was crying, and my aunt telling me I had a little brother."

This was the client's first report. When I began asking him questions, he went back and filled in a number of these pieces. This is fairly typical. It can be a signal that there are trust issues to explore with the client.

"The dock was full of people with white suits and black ties. And they were saluting and I wondered why they were getting on the big boat."

Most memorable aspect: Seeing my father on top of the ship on the side near us when it pulled away.

Feeling associated: "Confusion."

("The dock was full of people with white suits and black ties.")

THERAPIST: *Are you a person who enjoys being around people coming and going?*

CLIENT: *Yeah.* (The client was a cocaine dealer, who had traffic like this at his house regularly.) (Note that the color association was white, like his drug of choice. The fact that people remember colors and report them is significant; so are the colors they report.)

Determining Positive Intents for Using Chemicals:

THERAPIST: *What were your positive goals for using the chemicals?*

CLIENT: *To feel OK. To relax.* (If a person goes through life confused and frustrated over people leaving him/her, it is easy to see a need to feel relaxed and at ease.)

Additional Questions:

"Do you feel when you get close to people, or when people get 'on top' with you, that they will pull away?"

"Are you a jealous person?"
"Do you have trouble with intimacy?"
"Is life confusing for you?"
"Do you wind up confused when you take action?"
"Do you have a need to be in charge?"

Example 8

Client: White Male
Age: Early 60s
Addiction: Post-Traumatic Issues/Alcohol

"I was the youngest of all the children, the baby. I was 3 years old. I remember waking up and going into my parents room very early in the morning and climbing up on the bed in between both of them and falling back to sleep. I felt very safe and secure between them."

Most memorable aspect: "Being between 'em."

Feeling(s) associated: Security.

Here the client was supported and made to feel secure externally, by his parents. Since this was such a positive memory for the individual, the therapist began to look for later personal life traumas that may have preceded the addiction.

THERAPIST: *Did you enjoy being the center of attention?*

CLIENT: *Yes.*

THERAPIST: *Did something happen to you later in life that seemed to change your world?*

CLIENT: *Both my parents died in a one-month period a couple of years ago.*

THERAPIST: *Did your chemical use change after that occurred?*

CLIENT: *Yes, I began to use heavily after my father's death and while my mother was dying.*

THERAPIST: *What was your positive intent for using?*

CLIENT: *I medicated my pain. I wanted to feel good again.*

This client had major issues related to support. In fact, taking care of his dying mother was at least as traumatic for him as the actual death of his father, because not only did it mean his support was gone, but he was all of a sudden called on to provide support for someone else. And without his father, he had no one to support him. He lost his balance; or more accurately, he lost their balance.

When addicts reach out for a drug for support (most often alcohol or a depressant), they are seeking external support. Once they have ingested the drug, however, they feel supported internally. This is one area that can cause difficulties for the therapist in terms of identifying where the client sees the locus of control.

(*"I remember waking up and going into my parents' room. . . ."*)

You can see he took action to get the external support. He did the same thing in seeking alcohol and for much the same reason.

We have found that 16% of the addicted clients we work with have some traumatic experience in which they changed their perceptions or their actions. In this case, the client may not have changed his basic perceptions—he felt secure between his parents, and without them he felt insecure. The behavioral change that occurred was his seeking alcohol for his security. Both fit his pattern of looking outside himself for a source of security. When early memories are positive in orientation, look back to see if there is a change in perception or action.

It is worth noting that these memories may in fact change—both the memories themselves and one's perception of them—reflecting major personality shifts that occur over the course of an individual's lifetime. Keep in mind that here we are talking about *major* personality shifts, not hoping to change, promising to change, or even starting to behave as if we have changed. Such shifts are usually accompanied by a wholesale reordering of our attitudes, beliefs, and values, once we have accepted responsibility for all that we are.

Chapter 3

BATTLEFIELD FOR AN INTERNAL CONFLICT

To suffer one's death and be reborn is not easy.

Fritz Perls

With Perceptual Adjustment Therapy, we find that awareness is curative in itself—the same idea held by both Adler and Perls. Once individuals begin to become aware of their role in life and how they maintain that role, the role's purpose becomes clear and options come into their field of awareness. The single most important aspect of this new awareness is the option of choosing personal responsibility over the denial of responsibility.

This assumption of personal responsibility goes hand in hand with self-acceptance—probably the single greatest joy in therapy. To others, it is as if a light has come on inside of the individual; to the individual, it is as if the world has been lit. We often speak of the "light in someone's eye" or an eye's "twinkle," and this is much more than figurative happiness. This is real, and almost anyone working in this field knows it. In fact, we believe that it is a fair measure of how far someone is in his/her recovery process and the true joy that recovery offers. Just as you can see the frustration in the dry drunk process, you can easily observe the pleasure people experience in a healthy recovery process.

In Chapter 2, we looked at early childhood memories that held the key to understanding the positive intents behind early chemical use and abuse. The chemicals were used to drop personal role barriers or, as we so often hear, to help lower inhibitions and allow repressed desires and their accompanying assertive behaviors to emerge. The denial of oneself is reinforced by the chemical use, for the chemical is given responsibility for the behavior. Furthermore, the knowledge of how to reproduce these new behaviors and how to drop the old role is temporarily lost and only remembered under the influence of the chemical. All of this means that the individual can achieve a semblance of balance in his/her life, but it requires the influence of a substance.

So, the internal conflict that we see in chemical-abusing clients comes directly from a desire for balance. Of course, it is elusive, because these individuals are seeking balance backwards. That is, rather than openly confronting how they are repressing parts of themselves, they instead choose to deny reality, fighting to maintain their role in life and forcing themselves to fit into "their place," first in the family and later in society at large.

This desire to fit in and our unique ability to establish our place immediately leaves us with a void. The moment we choose one side we give up the other, and most often it is in direct competition with our siblings that we first do this.

Sibling rivalry over roles in families is so pronounced that with a minimum of training you can tell the difference between most children, whether they were firstborn, second-born, middle, youngest, or only children. The characteristics are obvious and distinctive, as are the roles that emerge in any addicted family—hero, scapegoat, mascot, and lost child—that Sharon Wegscheider-Cruse (1989, p. 85) pointed out in the '70s.

In many cases, the smaller the family, the more pronounced the competition between or among the children. This competition is nothing new, though we often choose to believe that things are getting worse. Can children really be more competitive than the Bible's "first" siblings, Cain and Abel?

In today's world, children may not resort to murder, but turf wars still start early. One child may be good in math and science while the other excels in language arts. Or one may show a talent for sports while the other achieves more in the classroom. This form of competition is one way that roles are chosen, established, and reinforced. The role sets up the denial of part of the child's self (the athletic part of an academically gifted child, the bookish part of an athlete), which sets up the void, the need to regain balance and wholeness. When the first use of a chemical resolves this internal conflict, a pattern of abuse and psychological dependency is likely.

THE INTERNAL CONFLICT

The external conflict over whether or not to use a chemical may not be that great in some situations. Our prevention efforts are making some headway and some social pressure exists to "Just Say No." Still, significant pressures to use remain among peers or family members who use, and we should note that prevention efforts have focused primarily upon street drugs like marijuana and cocaine. Television and the media continue to glamorize, normalize, and socialize the use of alcohol, so while social pressure is growing against other drugs, alcohol consumption among young people continues to rise throughout much of the country. Regardless, it is not the external agent that we have to deal with—if we can assist our clients in achieving integration and balance, that will take care of itself.

The following poem is one written by a young client. She provides us with a fascinating look at the internal conflict in her own life as she perceives it, including the ramifications it has upon her relationship with her parents.

YOU & ME

I know two people that don't want me to call them by their names;
because they only need You.
Me is very lonely.
Me tells you, "Hey! Please look at You!"
You says, "No. I'm scared."
Me says, "But what about me? I want to Be!"
You says, "Why should I?"
Me says, "Because I'm freezing in this cave—HELP ME PLEASE!"
You says, "I'm going to try for Me."
Me is frightened and screams, "Why did you do this to you?"
You says, "Because I didn't know what else to do!"
Me says, "Do you want me to help You?"
You says, "Yes, please show You, Me."
Me says, "Look in the mirror, beyond You."
And Me promises You that You will find Me.
You & Me ain't so bad after all.
You asked Me, "What about Mama & Daddy?"
Me said, "Stan & Gladys can take care of themselves."

The first part of the poem looks at the confusion and fear in most dependent individuals and identifies the clear division in her life. As the metaphor continues, both parts reach out to each other and embrace in an intimate moment—the onset of integration. Essential to this is the fact that in this moment, with greater personal awareness, she takes responsibility for her own actions instead of laying that responsibility on her parents. At the same time, she sets her parents free to live their own lives. This poem is wonderful as it shows us so clearly her confusion and her inability to express or accept her own "oneness."

Terminology

Previously, we have used the term *drunk* as a label for the chemical-using part of a dependent person instead of calling it by Perls' term, the ***bottom dog***. Similarly, we have used the phrase *dry drunk* for the ***top dog***. By changing names again, we hope to accomplish two goals: (1) to make the split clear for professionals working in treatment, as these were already well-understood "characters," and (2) to provide a definition (and hopefully, tools for treating) the legendary ***Dry Drunk Syndrome***.

While this language has been helpful in some cases, it becomes problematic as well. These terms carry such negative connotations in chemically dependent families that individuals have trouble identifying positive intents (let alone positive outcomes) arising from chemical use. The word "drunk" is such a negative auditory trigger that family members and users themselves immediately go into a negative emotional state as soon as a therapist uses it. Not only does it become difficult for them to see positives, they become downright negative and defensive. They become primed for a fight and quickly fall back into their most familiar roles, the closest thing to anything empowering that they have had. In short, a family-wide denial system sets up when you as a therapist use the word "drunk" to describe even a part of anyone present.

If you were setting out on a car trip, you wouldn't want to deflate the tires immediately before you left. Similarly, we as counselors should do our best to keep our clients "inflated" to the proper degree for travelling on their road to recovery. So, for the sake of our clients and their attitudes, let's label the top dog or dry drunk as the ***inactive*** side of the chemical abuser. Likewise, we can call the bottom dog or the drunk, the ***active*** side of the abuser.

Definitions: The ***inactive side*** is that part of a chemical abuser or chemically dependent person that desires to stay straight at all costs.

The ***active side*** is the part of a person who, though chemically free at the present time, wishes to use.

Each of these sides is representative of a "state of being"—each has distinct physiological characteristics that accompany its presence in the individual.

By paying careful attention to voice tone and tempo, posture, facial expressions, muscular flex, skin color, and breathing rate, a therapist can tell exactly which part is doing the talking in his/her client.

Spouses of chemically dependent persons are probably best at this, owing to years of training. Almost intuitively, they can sense which side of the individual, active or inactive, is present at a given moment. How many times have you heard a dependent client say, "My wife/husband even knows when I'm getting ready to use. For the life of me I don't know how she/he can tell"? Though it may seem like intuition, it is not; this is instead evidence of state-related affects, and the observation of them by a client's wife or husband.

In addition to the active and inactive states, there is a third—the *chemical state*. This is established when a mood-altering chemical has been taken by the client. Interestingly, the chemical state allows us to see clearly the positive in-tents underlying the client's use, for he/she will be acting them out. If the client is using to feel less afraid, he/she will be behaving bravely, sometimes aggres-sively. If he/she is using to be more sociable, you will see him/her actively engaging with others. Even if the setting is ludicrous, in a Detox unit, for example, the person will act in accordance with his/her positive intentions for use.

Of course, this is true only up to a point. If the client gets extremely high, the chemical itself takes over.

In the chemical state, the client usually knows precisely what his/her de-sired behaviors and feelings are—that is, he/she can tell you his/her positive intents for using.

We will now move into some excerpts of training before Perceptual Ad-justment Therapy was named. I suppose that I as a therapist existed with P.A.T. for years before it was named, much as Native Americans do with their children. Just as Native Americans often choose not to name a child as soon as it is born, but rather allow the child's name to emerge from its own existence, Perceptual Adjustment Therapy has shown itself to me to be exactly that. Only it took quite some time for me to discover it.

WORKSHOP EXCERPTS

The remainder of this chapter is an excerpt from a workshop that should give you a historical framework for P.A.T., as well as some clarity on the addiction recovery process and a few traps that P.A.T. can help identify and treat, such as the Dry Drunk Syndrome:

> **JIM HOLDER (JH):**   *We in this field are working with a very diffi-cult, very sick population. I think we do not fully understand the dis-ease that they suffer from, or what is going on with ourselves some of the time. And when we do not understand, we become irritated and angry and begin to feel like we are not successful. With so many ad-dicted people, feeling so down on themselves, believing that they can't accomplish things, their goal becomes to get you to give up on them too. And the minute you give up on them, then they say, "See, I'm not worth anything. Even my counselor believes I'm hopeless." So our goal is to stick it out with them on healthier terms. We have got to be human with them. Therapists get angry, and clients are used to people being angry with them. Some of the therapists whom they love the most are the ones who fuss and fight with them, because it is familiar and much more like what they are used to.*
>
> *There is a trap here, however. Many of these same counselors—cli-ents' "favorites"—are the ones who are agitating and confrontive. They talk aggressively in irritated tones of voice. They take a client's addic-tion personally, sometimes screaming at the client, attempting to force him/her into sobriety, much like the client's family has, but armed with treatment jargon. One telltale sign of this counseling trap will come from the client when, near the end of the treatment course, he/she says, "I'd like to thank my counselor for pulling it out of me," giving the credit for recovery to the counselor as if the client had nothing to do with what took place. Another sign is when one client says to another, "Get [so & so] for your counselor—they'll pull it out of you." Trans-lation: "With this person as your counselor, you won't have to be responsible for your recovery. They'll do it for you."*
>
> *As an aside, when clients use phrases like "pull it out of you," it is another red flag. I am reminded of the movie* The Exorcist—*as if the addict is disgorging a part of themselves, exorcising a demon, or simply giving up personal responsibility for his/her illness and recovery. The active side of someone's illness is not something to be cut out or de-stroyed; it is a legitimate, necessary part of who they are. Instead, we can identify its positive intents for use, then achieve the intents in healthier ways. This business of hating it only helps to perpetuate the game, for with it the client can continue clinging to his/her notions of helpless-ness, victimhood, worthlessness, or some other self-defeating idea.*

So two primary pitfalls are out there for us counselors—giving up and becoming negative. Today we are going to talk about how to be persistently positive.

CHEMICAL ABUSE COUNSELOR (CAC): *There is a client I have had for a long time. He will stay straight for a while and then relapse. He doesn't seem to have any tools to stay straight. He seems really good at sabotaging himself. When he comes in to see me, he will talk and really get in touch with his feelings. He talks about liking the way he feels in my office, that he can be real. But he says he can't take the good feelings out of the room, back into his everyday world with him. So how would you turn that into something positive?*

JH: *I wouldn't turn that into anything. I would do what he asked for. He gave it all to you. "I wish I could take this positive feeling out of the room." It's already positive. He has a goal—feeling good with another person—and he has successfully achieved it with you. Support it by asking what exactly those positive feelings are and how he accomplished them in your office. Be careful to keep the responsibility on him for his feelings, because he may be trying to turn them over to you. There's a trap that may be inferred from this, that you are the cause of his positive feelings. Just sidestep it and ask him what his strategy was for successful interaction with you. Then you can go about setting up situations where he can take those feelings out of the room. For example, find someone else in a nearby office or other area, and take him with you and have him sit down and talk to someone else. Not as a therapist, but as a person. Support him and encourage him to use the same strategy for interaction that he used with you, and he can carry positive feelings with him outside the office. This will allow him to begin realizing that his old belief system is untrue—that in fact he was changing his strategy for dealing with people when he left your office.*

Most of the time, on some level, the client will tell you what he wants.

Let me go on to another idea—that of the "split" we find in each of our clients. You are probably very much aware of this, the fact that within the client there is a part that wants to stop using chemicals and a part that wants to use. Sometimes, even clients themselves will identify it, making references like "my addict wanted to do so and so" or talking about their "alcoholic thinking." This is more often the case with people well on their way in recovery—people who have identified the split within themselves. Most clients we see are in internal conflict or they would not be coming to see us.

There are some easily identified patterns to this split, patterns that were first suggested by Fritz Perls back in the '60s. As we mentioned earlier, the "top dog" is the inactive state—an addicted person without the benefit of chemicals to cope with life. Usually, this part will be very authoritative, with very rigid rules about how the client should live, and how the therapist should live, what kind of therapist you should be, how the client's children should act, and so forth. Clients working from this state are extremely rigid in their belief systems and often exhibit mood swings.

The other part, the "bottom dog," is the Active state. Perls' "bottom dog" is more flexible, fun-loving, outspoken, affectionate, and rebellious. In our clients, the active state appears before a chemical is ever used. Probably the best identifiers for this state early in treatment are family members. They will say something like, "You are getting ready to get drunk. I know it." They can tell because when the active state appears, it completely replaces the inactive state. The person seems frustrated and is angry with himself/herself. This is because the active state hates the dry state and resents the harsh rule that the dry state usually places over the whole person. The active sees the inactive as being oppressive and always afraid. The active is saying, "I'm never giving up! I'm going to use until there's not a penny left, and I'm never stopping again. I crave adventure and nothing scares me now. I can take on anyone." This anger also can be used as a setup—when an argument ensues, the individual can storm out and go use.

Perhaps the primary distinction between these two halves is that they are almost always the opposite of one another. If one is shy and reserved, the other will be outgoing and assertive. It is the reconciliation and integration of these two halves that is the essential challenge the addict faces.

If you get a chance, talk to your clients when they are under the influence. Do not send them home when they are drunk. Talk to them. It is a terrific opportunity to learn something about the balance they are struggling for. You are getting an honest look at clients' desired behaviors. People say it is all "drunk talk." I say drunk talk is real. It is one of the ways people would like to be when they are sober, if not in the words themselves, then in the expression of those words.

When most people come to inpatient treatment on their own for help, they are desperate and they honestly want help. Not too surprisingly, many of them come in while they are drunk or high. Now ask yourself, "Which part brought them in?" When they walk in drunk, who is agreeing to get help? The chemical state! The chemical state is the one with the courage to change.

Two days later (same counselor, same client), the client denies all the feelings and actions and decides he/she does not need treatment and can handle things all by himself/herself. And the client leaves treatment. It is the inactive state that does not want help. The inactive says, "I can handle this. I don't need A.A. or N.A. I can do this on my own, just like my daddy did. If you are man enough, you can just stop, and I'm stopping."

The client fails to realize that when his daddy died, he died in a hospital from a heart attack. And his daddy had been miserable on a dry drunk for 15 years. Dry drunks die early. They go with heart disease, suicides, and other stress-related killers (probably many kinds of cancer and a host of compulsive disorders too).

Dry drunks are under enormous stress to be perfect, and they return the favor by insisting that the world be perfect as well. They have given up spontaneity, flexibility, and fun because that side of themselves causes embarrassment and shame. So they totally shut a part of themselves out. Or they try to, while the fear of impending doom lingers deep inside.

The splits know about each other. Not as they really are, of course, but as a Dr. Jekyll and Mr. Hyde effect. They have a fear of each other.

When the chemical state is active, it is totally active—absolutely, 100% in control. From the moment the chemical enters the body, it is as if the inactive state—the rigidly controlled part of the self—just sort of disappears.

According to John Grinder (1992), a study was conducted years ago using two groups of heroin addicts. The first went through a methadone maintenance program for six weeks; the second was told that it was, but was given a placebo instead. Both groups went through treatment together without any significant incidents. At the end of six weeks, after the necessary information had been gathered, the groups were

*had been done and which group was which. So what hap-
You guessed it. The placebo group went into withdrawal. So it
personal belief in the situation that is important. Simply planting
ea is enough to effect a complete change in an addicted person.*

what do we do with this person with two sides?

CAC: *Get them together!*

JH: *Okay, how? What does that mean?*

CAC: *You get balance in their lives, to start with.*

JH: *Good idea.*

CAC: *What about getting the person to recognize positive characteristics of each side? Then he/she could learn to accept the fact that he/
she has both. Get the person to identify the positive intents that each
side has, the underlying motives for the two behavior patterns.*

JH: *Exactly! You have just discovered the greatest benefit to identifying positive intents—it can defuse the anger and resentment that such
a person has toward himself/herself. It gives the person a starting point
for self-acceptance.*

*You see, until the person identifies the two sides and the positive in-
tents that each has, he/she just has this confusion and fear. The person
knows what he/she doesn't like about each side but doesn't know what
the other side is doing.*

*Whether anyone involved with the situation can see it or not, the ac-
tive part is trying desperately to save the person's life. It is not working, and it is misguided, but the active side is attempting to make more
of the person's life. So the active state tries, through the only means
available (chemicals that lower inhibitions), to introduce balance—even
if it is only on a part time basis, even if it is dangerous, and even to
the detriment of the person's material or social well-being. Of course
it doesn't work, but the important thing is the positive intent. The active side actually is trying to make life more enjoyable.*

CAC: *I can think of a number of drug and alcohol patients who,
once they sober up, are just like you describe. They get back into that*

street thing of denying their problems. It seems like they are embarrassed or ashamed, or can't acknowledge the denial itself.

JH: *One thing that can be helpful to identify is that the inactive state is also the codependent part. That is the part that was there before the person ever took a drink or a drug. As you know, many addicted people come from addicted families, either their immediate families or their extended families. Which is to say that basically, they come from rigid backgrounds. In a sense, codependency is the first part of the illness an individual usually experiences. It is primary, waiting for a chemical; then, when the chemical comes, the addiction becomes primary and the codependency becomes secondary, like a shadow.*

In inpatient treatment centers, we get a lot of validation for these ideas. You see a person come in, under the influence and sweetly reasonable. They say that they are ready to do anything to stop using and they ask for help. Within a few days, they are criticizing everything about the center—you, the other patients, the program, the food, everything. They are scared, scared they are going to have to go through the rest of their lives without any release for the repressed side of themselves, the active part. I can summarize the most important part of their treatment right here: that they may recognize this—that they are afraid of their active side and that they need to reintegrate that side of themselves into their lives.

They only will reach this awareness if they feel safe—that it is fine for them to be right where they are and that no one is passing judgement on them. Both parts of the person, the inactive and the active, need to get this message very clearly and begin to trust you, the therapist.

This is one of the reasons we use positive intents. Positive intents do not threaten either part of the person. Consider the active part's positive intents (Figure 3.1): "to relax," "to socialize," "to feel confident," "to have courage," "to feel complete." These are certainly good. Likewise with the inactive: "to be respected," "to be safe and secure," "to fit in well in the community." Is there anything really wrong with our clients' intentions?

CAC: *So in an inpatient setting, you train or teach people to see things differently, like you are doing here?*

JH: *Well, yes. At least initially. In treatment, we begin with just this kind of education so that people can have the awareness. But we also*

Active Side	Inactive Side
to relax	to be respected
to socialize	to be safe and secure
to feel confident	to fit in well in the community
to have courage	
to feel complete	
to be more outgoing	
to have fun	
to meet people of the opposite sex	

Figure 3.1.   Positive intents.

move into more experiential modes as well, like with role-playing and with therapy.

For example, I might begin by asking for a volunteer. The volunteer is probably going to have an emotional experience, because I am going to ask them to let the active side out when they are sober. And I get the rest of the group to help. Their job is to support me, and when they see this person change from the inactive to the active, or vice versa, they are going to say so if I miss it. Then we go through a role-play or hot-seat work with the client.

This is usually educational for those watching and therapeutic for the volunteer. The volunteer may be confused at the end, at least on a conscious level, but deep down, he/she is miles ahead because he/she has experienced it. In fact, if we succeed therapeutically, the client experiences relief, and everyone in the group usually knows it and appreciates it. This is the start of integration, though it is often marked by mixed feelings and confusion.

By definition, confusion must precede any new awareness.

When a group has seen someone have this experience, then it is a good time to begin some work with them on positive intents and goal-setting. You see, as they watch the volunteer, they can see more objectively the two sides and the motives underlying each. Ask them to take a piece of paper and make two columns labelled active and inactive. Have them write down the positive intents for each. Now looking at the lists that result, there are two things you can do.

The first is to use them as treatment goals for the client.

The second is to test the integration that has been achieved. For example, if one of the positive intents for the active part was "To be more outgoing," then you can test it right there in the group. Simply ask the volunteer if he/she can express that for the group somehow. If the client can accomplish the positive intents of the active side while sober, the integration work has begun.

Remember that each part of the person has a legitimate value. *Probably the biggest mistake we can make in the field is to label the active side of the client as "Bad." There is nothing bad about it. It is simply a real part of the person who is trying to express himself/herself and does not know any other way. Instead of acting differently toward a client who has just "slipped," for instance, we might look at it as though the active side had something it needed to tell us. When you see the active side, that is fine. Just know that you are about to get some new information about the person. You can even thank the active side. We as therapists need to trust that that is exactly what is happening, and that if for some reason we miss that piece, the active part will give us another opportunity to pick it up.*

Of course, the inactive part is not "bad" either. Sometimes, when a client achieves awareness of his/her positive intents, especially those of the active side, he/she may experience enormous guilt. Somehow it seems to the client that everything has blame associated with it; someone is responsible for everything, so he/she must be at fault for the addiction. Well, that is not entirely true. You want the client to assume some responsibility, but that is not what the client is likely to do. It probably will be all or nothing for the client. In this case, the client takes all the blame. And that is not productive. We are not looking for blame or trying to judge anyone. Group work can help a client see that you as a therapist appreciate people just for being themselves. At the same time, the client may begin to notice that his/her inactive side does not have all the answers and that it does not have complete awareness.

CAC: *I have a client who comes in sometimes sober, sometimes drinking, and is looking for his positive intents, and seems to be making some progress. But I became very concerned the last time we met when he was very intoxicated and driving. I had a real difficult time telling him to go home, but his response was to say that I was just like his mother. "You are trying to judge me," he said. I tried to be as positive as I could, but he has stayed away for three sessions. He's coming back this week, but I feel somewhat confused about what I should have done.*

JH: *Legally, we can't allow them to drive while drinking and not notify the authorities. It's that simple. As addiction counselors, we have a responsibility to protect our clients and others, especially in a life-endangering situation like driving. You can contact the authorities with-out breaking confidentiality—you don't have to say who you are, and you may not have to identify the individual by name.*

I like to give people choices when they come to see me and they are drinking and driving. I might say something like, "Would you rather call someone to come get you, have me help find someone to take you home, or go get behind the wheel of your car and I will call the police and they may put you in jail?" I have called the police before, but usually, if it is put to them that way, clients will make another choice. I don't have a big problem with clients coming in under the influence, but driving themselves there and back in that condition is another mat-ter. Depending on the client, of course, a trip to detox might be an option too. People need boundaries—we all do. And if one of our cli-ents demonstrates that he/she lost sight of boundaries, we are fulfilling our roles by making those boundaries clear to him/her.

CAC: *What about when someone comes in drunk in a group set-ting.*

JH: *With regard to the driving, I do pretty much the same thing. But with regard to the group work, it is a judgement call. There are so many things on which it depends. For example, when a client is under the influence, you have open access to the active side, and you can show it to whoever is in your group. At the same time, you do not want to exploit the person or drive him/her away. If you are doing a family group, it can be invaluable, because the chemical state will trigger responses in the family members that can serve as references for the rest of your work with them. But an intoxicated person can be abusive in such a setting too, and we want to avoid that. One thing to bear in mind is that intoxication is only useful provided the person isn't too far into the wind. You just have to use your judgement as to where that line should be drawn.*

CAC: *The other side of the coin is that I work in a center with very rigid rules. Those who come in under the influence have to leave. I have had people in my groups say that they had a drink or two before coming, and I know that they are looking to see if I am going to "love" them and "accept" them and change the rules so that they can stay or* *if I am going to be hard with them and stick by the rules. It is difficult for me in situations like that.*

JH: *If there are rules, I go by them. I think it is really important for our clients to know that there are rules and that we as therapists abide by them. You really can get into trouble when you make exceptions to the rules—if you fail the test, you may have two members drunk in your group the next week.*

CAC: *I did!*

JH: *The way I know is from experience too. Just like in most treatment programs, if you use while you are in the program, you are out of the program. A particularly difficult case comes to mind. This was with an adolescent who was in detox. Someone mailed him some acid, on a stamp, and he did it there in Detox. This was something hard for the staff to deal with. Some were saying he was "just" an adolescent, or that the program hadn't really begun for him, and that he hadn't had enough time to straighten up and know what he was doing. By the end of their struggle, though, they knew that he had to go. A contract had been made between us and the kid that he would not use, and he broke it. We really didn't have a decision to make.*

We had been cut out of the decision, but we had to accept that before we could let the logical consequences occur. We did refer him immediately to a more structured adolescent program. And we also had the client let his parents know where the acid came to him from—it was from his sister.

So it is extremely difficult when the test comes, but we need to show addicts that we care enough about them to honor our word and allow them to be responsible for their behavior. Alcoholics and drug addicts need the structure. They also need to be loved and cared for, and even when they sock us in the nose emotionally, we need to let them know we are still here without belittling them.

And they will make it difficult, especially when they go through life with a guiding fiction or perception that people will turn them away. They will set up the situation to make that happen or will set up even the opposite—that they always get their way. In treatment centers, guiding fictions will set a manipulative trap or test for the staff.

REFERENCES

Grinder, J. (1992). Workshop presentation, Southeast Center of Neuro-Linguistic Programming, Raliegh, NC.

Wegscheider-Cruse, S. (1989). *Another chance: Hope and health for the alcoholic family.* Palo Alto, CA: Science and Behavior Books.

Chapter 4

STATE DEPENDENT LEARNING: A SCIENTIFIC EXPLANATION FOR THE INTERNAL CONFLICT

The time has finally arrived for clinicians and researchers to join forces, for both have a great deal of knowledge to offer one another. Perceptual Adjustment Therapy incorporates theory from both in its clinical strategies. In this chapter we will look at some of the scientific underpinnings of P.A.T. In many workshops, the question is asked, "How many counselors have an understanding of state dependent learning or state dependent recall?" Usually fewer than 10% of the participants will acknowledge an understanding of the terms, yet this information is critical to understanding the nature of chemical dependency.

Let us start by discussing the definitions and characteristics of dependency. The new definition of alcoholism recently developed by the American Association of Addictive Medicine and the National Council on Alcoholism and Drug Dependency as stated in *The Counselor* (November/December, 1992) is

> Alcoholism is a primary chronic disease, with genetic psycho-social and environmental factors influencing its development and manifestation. The disease is often progressive and fatal. It is characterized by impaired control over drinking, preoccupation with the drug alcohol, use of alcohol despite adverse consequences, and distortion

of thinking, most notably denial. Each of these symptoms may be continuous or periodic. (p. 6)

These characterizations of alcoholism are also true for other addictions and compulsive behaviors, including narcotics, food, gambling, sex, and a host of others.

Understanding and breaking down the characteristics as they relate to scientific research will be helpful—it was extremely relevant in the development of Perceptual Adjustment Therapy. P.A.T. was developed primarily through clinical observation over two decades. In recent years, and especially in recent months, there has been increasing scientific influence. The key phrases in the definition with regard to state dependent learning are *impaired control, distortion of thinking,* and *denial.*

Denial is the most notable case in which there is thought distortion. Much of this distortion comes from the client's inability to remember or learn when not under the influence of his/her chosen addiction. Simply put, knowledge acquired during periods of intoxication is lost or barely remembered during periods of sobriety. This might include knowledge or behaviors such as the ability to speak up, relax, or share feelings with others—things that become positive intents for use in the chemically dependent person. So the new skills acquired during intoxication seem to be lost, since learning and recall are hampered.

In a recent workshop, I mentioned to the participants that many addicted individuals in treatment say that they have never danced sober in their lives. One therapist then described a dance held in a treatment center. She said the people who had left the treatment center and were alumni came back and they danced just a little, while the people who were in the second phase of their program and were sober did not dance at all. Then, when the detox clients came to the dance, they "tore the floors up." That is primarily because the people who were in a chemical state had full recall of the dance steps they had learned while they were accomplishing their positive intents (i.e., socializing, relaxing, having fun, meeting people of the opposite sex).

LEARNING AND RECALL

Research validates that information learned in one chemical state is best retained or remembered in the same chemical state. In *Drug Discrimination and State Dependent Learning,* Weingartner (1978) showed clearly that cigarette smoking has state specific affects on memory, as do other drugs researched. In this study, Weingartner took 32 smokers who averaged 15.2 cigarettes per day, and these individuals were selected randomly and assigned to four separate test groups. Each of the four groups spent 15 minutes studying a 555-word article. Then they took a 10-minute break before the test. The scores were as follows: 4.1 correct answers for the eight subjects who smoked during the study and during the test, 2.6 correct answers for the eight subjects who smoked while studying and not while they took the test, 3.6 correct answers for the subjects who were smoke free or nicotine free during studying and during the test, and 2.9 correct answers for the eight subjects who smoked only during the test. The outcome was obvious even for those of us who are not researchers. Those persons who studied and tested in the same state made higher scores than those who studied and tested in different states.

Think for a moment of how many of our clients smoke heavily. And with the emphasis there is on not smoking in governmental buildings, hospitals, and treatment centers, many of our clients are not smoking during group sessions—the very groups in which we, as clinicians, have designed to teach them how to live drug free lifestyles. So they are going to discover new positive ways to interact, new ways to assert themselves, new ways to share their feelings without the use of chemicals; yet, when they leave treatment and go out into the real world, more than likely they are smoking in many of these situations. The very things we have just taught them—the breakthroughs in awareness they have made—may not be remembered or may be remembered vaguely. On the outside the persons will be in a chemical state of nicotine use; when they acquired the information, they were in a drug free state at least for a portion of the education or therapy group.

FEAR, MEDICATION, AND LEARNING

Studies on fear have shown that Benzo-diazepenes, used to reduce fear, cause an individual to lessen fear while in a chemical state, and then to have reduced memory retention when no longer on Benzo-diazepenes. Yet detox centers (which usually employ Benzo-diazepenes in managing withdrawal symptoms) also put individuals into education groups or individual sessions with counselors. Many of us know that as inpatient programs have shortened their length of stay to assist with managed care and to market their programs to managed care organizations, these inpatient settings have intensified their programs and have much more education and counseling occurring in the detox center. Now, however, research is showing that a lot of the information that we are giving these individuals in education and therapy sessions is not going to be remembered. Unless we change what we teach in detox, our quality of care will be reduced for the sake of marketing, and the same managed care systems seeking to lower health-care costs will eventually defeat their own purpose with recidivism.

Back in the mid-1970s, I was a detox counselor. One morning I had a session with a lady who was fairly new in the detox unit, and the two of us had what seemed to be a very warm and genuine session full of awareness, where the patient seemed to get a clear understanding of her addiction. The following day when I saw the lady for a second session, she had lost the wonderful awareness she had gained in our previous session. To my dismay, she had no recollection of me whatsoever. Her lack of memory prompted me to go into the detox unit and look through the chart to see what medication she had been given. My confusion was soon lifted when I saw in the chart that she had been given a rather excessive amount of Valium during her first days in detox. The medical team that had given that amount of Valium had all good intentions of helping this patient; however, in this case they defeated their own purpose. The nice thing in remembering this is that it was not long before the entire unit reduced its use of medications to a level of preventing seizure, but little else. It is funny, but this lady can probably still remember the awareness she got when she was in my office. The only problem is she would need to be stoned on Valium to recall it.

With an understanding of state dependent learning, counselors can change their priorities in a detox settings and in other programs in which individuals may be under the influence of prescription medication. You may want to keep your words of wisdom as a counselor for a time that is truly appropriate. When individuals are in a chemical state, we need to educate them on those things that would be important for them to know and understand and recall when they are under the influence of that chemical. For example, you may want them to become aware of the number of positive reasons to stop using as soon as they start. If they do use, you want them to remember to call their sponsor or professional to get immediate help. You see, we do not need to throw our hands up and just say, "Good golly, I'll quit!" We need to think rationally about those things that individuals need to understand and recall under the influence. So our objective changes. When the person is chemical free in another part of the program, or in an outpatient program, we can educate that client with specific information he/she needs to know when he/she is chemically free, to remain chemically free, and to live a fuller life.

DENIAL AND FAMILY INTERVENTION

It is imperative that professionals understand different forms of denial. The first form of denial, which we discussed in Chapter 2, comes when an individual begins to deny parts of himself/herself long before chemicals are used. The second type of denial is that of addictive denial, where the denial may be a direct conscious lie.

Denial, according to *Webster's Ninth Collegiate Dictionary*, is the refusal to admit the truth or reality. For decades, in the field of addictions treatment, we have treated all denial in a similar manner. We seem to be very confronting and accusatory in our efforts to break through the denial, but I wonder if that is the best method when the client is incapable of remembering his/her actions. This third form of denial we might call *state dependent denial*. With a better understanding of it, we might confront or accuse our clients less, realizing that they actually have no recall. Our goal is to find ways to help them learn about their behaviors, their actions, and their character when they are under the influence.

A method for accomplishing this may be found in the Johnson Institute form of family intervention, where the family comes in with the individual, and lets him/her know about things that have happened while the person was under the influence and the way they have felt about these things. This gives the straight alcoholic/addict a chance to visualize himself/herself in an intoxicated state and to experience the emotion and the consequences for those behaviors. One of these consequences would be to realize the pain that the family has been feeling for such a long time so that the individual will have a memory. It may be a memory that he/she has just developed, but from that day forth the person will have a memory that he/she can go back to when wanting to use chemicals. The most positive side of this is that the person will also have a memory of how much his/her family loves him/her and yearn for family congruency.

Goodwin et al. (1986), found that an individual has a relative inability to transfer information obtained during sobriety to periods of intoxication. When the individual is intoxicated, he/she in a sense forgets the consequences faced while intoxicated. This research by Goodwin et al. helps explain some of the characteristics of addiction, such as continued use of a chemical after adverse consequences. Well, if the individual has no memory of the consequences for his/her behavior, then it is as if the consequences do not exist anyway. So we as clinicians have to help the individual establish memory of these consequences, and Johnson Institute family interventions are the most proven method for accomplishing this.

If you are not using family therapy in your treatment process, then you are missing the boat. You are giving up one of the prime opportunities you have to get through to the chemically dependent person. Family interventions are not

Figure 4.1.   Schematic to show that what is learned at any point along the continuum will be best remembered at or near the same point or state.

simply to get an individual into treatment—for the family to sit down and go through the discussion portion of an intervention with the person in treatment is one of the most powerful things I have ever witnessed, because this builds memories for the addicted person. The family builds memories that are tied so closely to emotions that the individual may never forget the memories while straight.

In closing, let us put out a safety net. If, after this discussion, you have missed the basic concept of state dependent memory, try a different way of looking at it. Imagine a continuum (Figure 4.1), and on the ends there are two kinds of memory retention: one is complete retention in a sober state, and the other is an alcoholic blackout. Now consider the continuum between these two states—everything in between is state dependent memory. Can you imagine that anything learned at any point along the continuum will be best remembered at that same point? It may not have to be at *exactly* that point to be remembered (for example, having just a few beers may bring a better recall of events that were barely remembered sober), but the closer the better. This might mean that someone actually could recall a "blackout"—the only catch being that the person would have to be at or near a blackout again in order to remember it. Of course, once the person was sober, he/she would not be able to recall the recall either.

REFERENCES

The Counselor. (1992, November/December). New definition of alcoholism developed. *The Counselor*, p. 6.

Goodwin, D. W. et al. (1986, May). Individual differences in state-dependent retrieval effects of alcohol intoxication. *Journal of Studies on Alcohol, 47*(3), 243.

Weingartner, H. (1978). Human state dependent learning. In D. T. Ho, B. W. Enchmund, & D. L. Chute (Eds.), *Drug discrimination and state dependent learning* (pp. 361–382). New York: Academic Press.

Chapter 5

SETTING POSITIVE
TREATMENT GOALS

The first obstacle we must traverse is that of the disease itself, with denial and delusions being parts of the disease. We have discussed delusional thinking and how it connects to state dependent recall. We also have discussed the denial the client has from early childhood, when the client chooses to deny parts of the self in developing his/her personality.

In this chapter, we want to grasp the idea that early memories are a metaphor for the individual's life. This metaphor explains the existence of the delusional thinking itself. For once an individual believes life is a specific way, he/she begins denying other possibilities.

The second major problem professionals have is one of their own perceptions, projections, and denial, and how these affect obtaining important information in the assessment of clients and their families. This problem is one established by clinicians themselves and can be seen in many common practices in the field today. Clinicians are constantly projecting their beliefs onto their clients, just as clients take in information and filter it to fit their guiding fictions. Clinicians do the exact same thing; therefore, clinicians need to guard against this common practice through their own personal awareness. In the process of gathering information, we must put clients in charge of which information is important to the therapeutic process.

QUESTIONING

We want to *keep clients in the here and now* in relation to their present situation. Otherwise, we dwell in the past seeking large amounts of fluff information. Gathering this information brings the counselor to the foreground and makes him or her the influencing force in the therapy process. *When the counselor becomes the influencing force, the client is stripped of responsibility and dignity.* As a counselor, you may believe you know the best way to guide the client, while in actuality, you lead the client into the past by asking specific questions, many of which may be irrelevant to the client's specific presenting problem.

For example, if you ask individuals if their parents beat them or whipped them severely as children, that would force individuals to come up with memories that could answer that specific question. The main problem is that what we asked may not be something of great importance to the client at this time. It may be something of an issue for the counselor, and perhaps something on which the counselor may need to work. In fact, we believe clients will lead us directly to the appropriate information if we will allow them to guide us instead of us interfering with the process. We believe that the few questions we are required to ask may best be held until the end of the assessment.

An example of one of these questions is one that concerns harm to self or others. For example, "Are you having thoughts of harming yourself or anyone else?" These important ideas would be brought out by the client if the ideas held any relevance to the client's presenting problem. In fact, we believe that after asking what the presenting problem is, questions need to be open-ended to avoid leading the client, allowing them to stay in the here and now. We would start off with questions like, "Tell us your first memory." This form of question gives clients control of content without influencing their thought process. It also allows them to talk to us on both conscious and unconscious levels.

The wonderful thing about this process is that clients soon understand they are in a partnership with the counselor in the healing process. When counselors ask specific questions of the past, they may be leading the client away from the presenting problem. At the same time, the counselor is defining the importance of each question by the way he/she places it in the list of questions, the way he/she asks the question, the tone of voice he/she uses, and the words he/she chooses to put inflection on (actual vocabulary in each sentence). The counselor quite often could end up with a goal that would be much more appropriate for himself/herself than for the person sitting in front of him/her.

In treatment teams, you can see this clearly when specific questions arise over and over again from one particular counselor. When this occurs, counselors are projecting their ideas onto the situation. Think for a moment of a male counselor who may have had severe problems in relating to his own father. This counselor will be the very one to bring that issue up in a treatment team meeting or will ask a question during an assessment process that will guide the client. It is no wonder that JCAHO (Joint Commission on Accreditation of Healthcare Organizations) inspectors find so many treatment programs and counselors lacking individualized treatment plans. The inspectors have difficulty telling one client's treatment plan from another.

So truly the time is here to put our clients first in the assessment process. We may put them in group therapy, where a lot of theories and common practice let clients take charge of their own group process. We may put them in individual and family sessions and let them discuss things and work some issues out on their own with us giving as little guidance as possible to accomplish the task. Likewise, it is time for us to put the client first in the assessment. Then the entire treatment process can be more centered on the client's needs instead of the counselor's needs or, in some cases, the program's needs.

METAPHORICAL VALUES IN MEMORY

As was stated earlier, we need to ask open-ended questions like, "What's your first memory?" to give the client more control. It is quite common that earlier memories from childhood actually may not have existed at all. Counselors need to keep that in mind when doing the assessment and *attend to the metaphorical value of the memory rather than any factual basis.* Whether something truly happened or not is not as important as the way a person perceives the event. Remember, these early memories are nothing more than a metaphor for life, and you can look in great detail at the memory, discovering this individual's path through life.

The process is as important as the content because they both come from the same metaphor. So, metaphorically, you can look at each specific thing in a memory, each word for example, or you can look at the overall picture that the first memory paints. The content pieces will give you specific information about the individual and smaller details in his/her life—the color green related in a memory may be relevant to their present life—while the process picture of the memory may show you how the individual thinks he/she needs to walk through life—a dangerous episode in the memory may suggest that today the individual puts himself/herself in dangerous situations.

It does not matter if he/she tells a lie about the first memory, because even in the lie, perceptions will be evident. Memories are either made up, filled in, or changed in some way to fit the person's perception of the world. That is the reason that if you ask siblings about similar memories, each one will give you a different account of what happened at that time. You will find different content and process information.

Our clients have a tremendous need to satisfy us, to tell us what they think we want to hear. I know I have had clients on numerous occasions seem slightly confused in sessions. When I asked them what the confusion might be, they stated that they were not sure what I was wanting to hear. So clients do wish to please us as therapists. We have to take this into account. Those clients who look for authorities to tell them how to live their lives will, if they think they have an indication of what we think is right, lean in our direction.

This desire to please counselors may be setting up some interesting problems in the field. Many people in recovery or in treatment today have been involved in sexual abuse or incest. This is so common that we have a tendency to look for these problems. We have to be very careful when we look for anything specific in an assessment because it is too often that we lead the client to find exactly what we look for, especially when we are running under the assumption that it is probably there. We will talk more about this in Chapter 6.

ASSESSMENT AND GOAL-SETTING

Once the clinician has assessed the level of dependency and the appropriate mode of treatment has been chosen—whether it is detox, inpatient, intensive-outpatient or outpatient—the clinician still needs to continue the assessment in order to establish appropriate individualized treatment goals.

Setting positive treatment goals is a vital proposition for any treatment process. Research has shown that goal development has increased the effectiveness of treatment. Goals obviously need to be in direct response to the assessment compiled by the client and the professional. As you know by now, a great deal of the responsibility and the focus on the goals need to be through the client. Whether the client is an individual or a family member asking for help with some specific problem in the individual's life, it is necessary for clients to have a great deal of influence on the goal-setting process so that the goals will relate directly to their needs.

In a management course in which I took part a few years ago, the presenter claimed that if you would write down a goal once, you ran a 75% chance of accomplishing that goal. If you would write down a goal daily until its accomplishment, your percentage would jump to a 95% accomplishment rate. Hearing this, I thought that the projected rate might be rather high until I began to practice it myself.

Let us look at the way successful people use their Daytimers (appointment calendars); one of the main objectives of the Daytimer is to get you to think about and write on paper what you need to accomplish that day and keep it until these things are accomplished. So when people take a morning devotional time, when they focus on one particular part of their lives on which they would like to have a positive outcome, that focus each morning most often will help them accomplish whatever it is they seek.

Setting positive goals is a therapeutic process in itself. Clients begin to develop an understanding of how they observe life, whether negative or positive. They become aware of their past positive intents for chemical abuse and ways they have chosen to observe the world. All of this will bear directly on the goals and objectives of each client.

There are five counseling stages to travel through in order to set up and accomplish goals: (1) socialization and building rapport; (2) understanding the presenting problem; (3) determining positive intents; (4) acquiring early memories and relating them to the problem; and (5) establishing goals and objectives based upon positive intents. There are times when you may skip over the first of these stages; however, we have found it to be counterproductive in the long haul. Therefore, I encourage you to stay with the stages as we show them to you.

There are two parts to goal-setting: first, the use of early memories to acquire the client's guiding fictions and perceptual filters, and second, the establishment of the positive intents of the client's active and inactive states. These may be accomplished through individual therapy, edu-therapy groups, homework, and/or any combination of the preceding. Once the positive intents have been expressed and listed, it is important to match them against the early memories to see if supporting evidence exists to verify the intents. For example, if the positive intent is to trust and feel special with a woman, and the first memory is having a toy taken away by a young girl, then you can see the congruence between the intent and the memory.

WORKSHEETS

You may wish to use homework forms like those shown in Figures 5.1 and 5.2 to acquire the positive intents from your client. Patience is vital for the clinician since clients usually have gotten into a pattern of looking for negatives instead of positives or looking for what they do not want instead of what they do want.

The worksheet in Figure 5.1 can be used to help clients identify their positive intents for their inactive part. Time will be needed to complete the worksheet; therefore, the worksheet can be used a homework between sessions.

Figure 5.2. can be used to provide a format for clients to use as they identify their positive intents for their active part. It, like Figure 5.1., requires time and probably can be homework for clients between sessions.

When clients have a serious problem with positive intents from the beginning, you may wish to give them a checklist (Figure 5.3) for them to complete prior to the next session. Then you can go over the list in your next individual or group session. It also may be valuable in family group to show various perspectives on behaviors. Use the behaviors or feelings checked to arrive at the positive intents. The reason we do not suggest using this first is that it does have the potential for leading the client.

Once positive intents have been established for the active and inactive parts, you have your goals identified, for your goals are to establish these positive intents chemically free. Your next step is to determine objectives for assisting your client in accomplishing these goals. Of course, these objectives will differ greatly depending on the modality of treatment (inpatient, outpatient, etc.). When the positive intent for chemical use was: "to share feelings with a member of the opposite sex," your objectives would be very different for an individual in an inpatient setting from a person in an individualized outpatient setting.

Positive intents *are* the goals. Objectives are simply the precise, measurable methods by which your client will accomplish these goals. In Figure 5.4 is an example of a plan a client and counselor developed for the active state's positive intents.

INACTIVE PART—The part of me that wants to stay straight.

My Positive Intents for staying straight are (Remember, a positive intent is always something you want *to accomplish or do*, not something you want to stop doing.):

1. _____

2. _____

3. _____

4. _____

5. _____

6. _____

7. _____

8. _____

9. _____

Is there anything wrong with wanting to accomplish these positive intents? Place a check by each of them that you would be willing to accomplish chemically free.

Figure 5.1. Worksheet for identifying my positive intents for my inactive part.

ACTIVE PART—The part of me that wants to use chemicals.

My Positive Intents for using chemicals in various circumstances are:

Situation   Positive Intent for Using Chemicals

1. _____   _____

2. _____   _____

3. _____   _____

4. _____   _____

5. _____   _____

6. _____   _____

7. _____   _____

8. _____   _____

9. _____   _____

Is there anything wrong with wanting to accomplish these positive intents? Place a check by each of them that you would be willing to accomplish chemically free.

Figure 5.2.   Worksheet for identifying my positive intents for my active part.

DIRECTIONS: Place a check on the line that indicates whether you tend to experience each item under the influence or not. Feel free to leave blank any items you are unsure of.

USING	STRAIGHT		USING	STRAIGHT	
____	____	Outspoken	____	____	Mean
____	____	Quiet, Reserved	____	____	Caring
____	____	Outgoing	____	____	Angry
____	____	Shy	____	____	Cheerful
____	____	Tense	____	____	Trusting
____	____	Relaxed	____	____	Suspicious
____	____	Excited	____	____	Critical
____	____	Calm	____	____	Encouraging
____	____	Emotional	____	____	Sociable
____	____	Hide Feelings	____	____	Withdrawn
____	____	Courageous	____	____	Punctual
____	____	Fearful	____	____	Tardy
____	____	Extroverted	____	____	Pampering
____	____	Introverted	____	____	Punitive
____	____	Boisterous	____	____	Carefree
____	____	Timid	____	____	Responsible

Figure 5.3. Checklist for use by clients who have serious problems with identifying positive intents.

Active State's Positive Intents:

1. To share feelings (alcohol)
2. To socialize (alcohol)
3. To relax when alone (marijuana)

Treatment Goals:

1. To Share Feelings
   a. Objective: Share my feelings once daily in group.
   b. Objective: Write a letter to my wife sharing my feelings at least twice this week.
   c. Objective: Share my feelings with a resident or staff-person who is not in my group.
2. To Socialize
   a. Objective: Involve myself in a card game with the residents at least twice this week.
   b. Objective: Involve myself in the Friday volleyball game.
   c. Objective: Sit and talk with a person I do not know in the next two days.
3. To Relax When Alone
   a. Objective: Begin a morning devotion and relaxation time.
   b. Objective: Learn and practice a relaxation technique each evening before going to sleep.
   c. Objective: Sit outside enjoying the outdoors and using relaxation techniques at least three times this week.

Figure 5.4.   An example of a plan a client and counselor developed for the client's active state's positive intents.

Chapter **6**

MEMORIES AS METAPHORS

The hardest thing in a counselor's work is leaving the client in charge.

An interesting problem is beginning to arise around memories. Of course, like so many problems, two sides to it exist. There have been many professionals looking at childhood memories as absolute, rather than as metaphors, and they have begun to act upon them as gospel. In cases of physical abuse, sexual abuse, and incest, counselors have had numerous clients confronting families with events that may never have happened at all.

Harold Lief has talked about the dangers of, and the numerous occasions when he believed people had, false memories about sexual abuse, many of which may had been encouraged by the counselor. When asked whether taking a skeptical attitude toward these memories, even if false, would tend to undermine the counselor and client relationship, Lief (Peck, May–June, 1993) replied

> Of course, the counselor wants to establish a therapeutic alliance and give the client the feeling that they are on the same wavelength. The problem arises, however, when counselors overtly ask the question, "Were you ever sexually abused as a child?" There is a risk in this situation that the client will be vulnerable to suggestions and remember the actual event. The validity of this response is questionable. (p. 21)

Lief pointed very accurately to the heart of the problem professionals have in obtaining early memories. And not only is it true in sexual abuse, I believe

69

counselors do that across the board with a majority of the questions they ask clients. I think we are guiding clients to areas that hold the greatest degree of importance to us.

It is not that sexual abuse is not a serious crime—it is. However, the ramifications of reporting and dealing with sexual abuse go beyond the scope of what is required for Perceptual Adjustment Therapy to use an early memory. When treating an early memory as more than metaphor, the memory of it must be extremely accurate and reality-based, and we have to be very careful how we proceed in helping the client work through his/her trauma and grief. Also, we must be certain that when sexual abuse did occur, that it is of prime importance to the client before we make it number one on our list of priorities in the treatment process. There are times that it is not the primary problem of the client, and therefore we do not need to make it primary, because if we do, we are stepping over our boundaries at that time.

FALSE MEMORY SYNDROME

Some time ago, a group of individuals in Philadelphia began to talk about the number of clients that they had who seem to have memories about sexual abuse that were not true. As they began to discuss this, they were amazed at the number of false accusations, and from this group, the *False Memory Syndrome Foundation* was established in Philadelphia. Since that time, the Foundation has heard from more than 5,000 family members who believe that one of their family members has had false memories. The Foundation also has developed terminology for individuals who have had problems with this. For example, "returners" are those people who, at some point, resume communication with their families. "Retractors" are those individuals who have disavowed the memories of abuse and acknowledged such ideas as false memories. The foundation has set up a newsletter and also gives out other information to individuals who would like it. In this information, there are numerous stories of retractors, returners, and other family members who have had problems. There are also stories of professionals who have seen problems arise from various therapeutic techniques, and the group also has attacked many of the theories and practices used in therapy. As a professional, I do believe we need to take a much closer look at ourselves and the way we obtain information. I agree that therapists have projected their own beliefs on their clients for years. As clients search for the "whys" to explain their lives and the problems they are having, they eagerly grasp these projections from counselors.

Clients desperately want to understand "why," as if it will hold the answer to their woes. In reality, "how" is the only word that will help them understand the maze they have internalized. Once a maze is understood, a person may in fact walk the avenues of the maze in great pleasure. Recently, I was at a county fair with some friends and their families. Visiting the different rides, our children dashed into the "Hall of Mirrors," which as you know is a very elusive maze to the first-timer. My 11-year-old had been in this very maze for several consecutive years. Now that he understands how it works, he has very little trouble moving through the maze. One of my friend's children, who had not had the same number of experiences and did not know how it worked, thought he saw the exit. As he stepped forward, he hit one of the mirrors so hard with his forehead that the vibration shook the front of the building. His parents and I were amazed by the force of the impact.

"Why" the mirrors are placed as they are made no difference whatsoever to the young man here—what was important was "how" the mirrors were positioned and a basic understanding of the fact that mirrors are illusory. Once he understands that, he can enjoy this event, and it will not be such a painful experience for him (or such a startling one for his parents). I dare say he probably will go through the maze with much greater ease in future years, now that he knows how it works.

Our job, as therapists, is not to solve clients' problems, but to help them understand how they see the world and how they reestablish things as they see them. Recently, I was conducting a workshop on the use of early memories. In the workshop were two charming ladies from New York. When I brought up the *False Memory Syndrome Foundation*, one of them became some-what upset and shared a great deal of concern about what was happening as a backlash of the Foundation. She reported that a client of hers, who had worked on some sexual abuse issues and had made much progress, became much more adept in dealing with day-to-day living. After hearing individuals from the *False Memory Syndrome Foundation*, however, the client believed his memories must really be false and, in fact, that he was crazy. At that time, he regressed rather quickly and lost his ability to function in daily life as well as he had.

This therapist did not disagree entirely with the Foundation. Quite the contrary, she almost jokingly made reference to another therapist who believed that any time a client put his/her hands over his/her lap, it meant the client was trying to hide sexual abuse. So her concern was not that the Foundation did not have some appropriate concerns, and she agreed that there were clients who were diagnosed as sexual abuse who were in fact not. Her concern was that individuals listening, who had actually been sexually abused and had memories of this, would think that they were false memories and, like her client, would regress in their healing process.

So we seem to have a "catch-22" on our hands. I think that FMS Foundation is correct—that clients are eager to listen to professionals and will grasp projection by the professionals. The trouble that I see is that the Foundation in turn may have the same impact on people as those counselors. These people are vulnerable, in many cases, and they are grasping for answers. Whether it is a therapist attempting to help someone (inadvertently misleading the client) or the FMS Foundation wanting to help someone by telling these stories of false memories (influencing the client to distrust themselves), in either case, the same thing can happen.

The answer lies in the fact that there simply is not a villain in this situation. Both sides have those who are attempting to help people accidentally causing people to move into even more trauma. The solution lies in the fact that we are always looking for "why" and not "how."

MEMORIES AS METAPHORS

We must learn to look at memories as metaphors and begin to understand how the individual sees life and how the individual interprets his/her memory so that we may help each from that point of view. In that case, we will be helping the individuals understand themselves and understand how they walk through life; then clients will be back in charge again with the responsibility of owning the way that they see things, instead of professionals and others taking that responsibility from them. So I hope the FMS Foundation will continue to do the work they are doing to help us understand false memories, and yet, I want them to be very careful about how they give out this information to the public so that they will not cause people with legitimate memories to think that those memories are inaccurate. I encourage therapists to keep working to help their clients through these terrible issues and to find ways of doing therapy that will allow clients to guide us to what is important in their lives.

Some of my clients have had a false memory, and I, myself, have had at least one false memory. I remember working at our farm when I was about seven years old. I had stayed home from school that day to help mow hay. We did not have a tractor. We had a mule-drawn rake—the type you usually only see in front of antique stores now. As I was driving the mule, raking the hay in nice rows, I remember seeing the school bus driving down the dirt road and the dust coming up behind it. As the school bus passed with my friend on it, I threw my hand up and waved at the kids. I remember feeling very proud, like I was doing a man's work that day. About 10 years ago, I shared that early childhood memory with some of my family members sitting in my father's farmhouse. As I finished the memory, my father assertively spoke up and said, "Jimmy," with a smile on his face and a gleam in his eye, "you know I would have never let you stay home from school to work." Then he chuckled a little. I paused momentarily and smiled while replying, "Yes, sir. I'm sure you're right." Accurate or not, I do love that memory. It is one of my fondest, so I think I'll just keep it.

You see, the reality of the memory is not really as important as the meaning the metaphor carries for me—the "how" in how I see things: my work is important for me in my life. And in keeping with my "memory," it is still important to me that my peers see me working—so today as a trainer, I am living my "memory" out.

LEAVING THE CLIENT IN CHARGE

As a final note on this subject, perhaps all of us as therapists need to be more careful in choosing which questions we ask and how we establish the importance of the answers. The hardest task in a counselor's work is leaving the client in charge.

This reminds me of the story of the frog who came into the counselor's office. The counselor, being a kind, concerned counselor, asked the frog exactly what he wanted. He said, "What can I do for you?" The frog replied, "When I hop, I seem to bump my butt, and it's become a problem because my butt's becoming rather sore now, because it happens practically every time I hop." When the counselor looked at this frog, he had forgotten his work for a moment because he noticed how ugly the frog was. The counselor thought, "My goodness! What an ugly frog." At that time, the counselor reached back and pulled out of his bag of tricks, a most wonderful treatment strategy. As he worked with the frog, the most magical thing happened—the frog turned into a handsome prince. When the prince appeared, the counselor sat back and smiled, but the prince glared at the counselor. Puzzled by this, the counselor said, "What's wrong?" The prince said, "Who do you think you are? I came in to you with the problem of bumping my butt when I hopped, and you changed the way I look. I liked myself as a frog, and you had no right to do what you just did!"

So as we work with our clients, let us remember we are working for them and not for our own egos. For truly, who are we to decide "how" our clients should be?

REFERENCE

Peck, R. (1993, May–June). Confronting the false memory. *Addiction & Recovery, 13*(3), 21.

Chapter 7

THE WISDOM
OF THE ALMIGHTY

Perhaps the following story will serve as a useful metaphor for integration and the appreciation of opposites.

> *There was a time even before time when the Almighty was all that existed and He grew very lonely. After being lonely for some time, He felt He may create something new in His experience. Then He imagined a brilliant illumination, and being pleased with His vision, He did in fact want to create it. The Almighty reached within Himself and drew some illumination from within His brilliance. It was magnificent, and He chose to call the brilliant illumination "Light." (See Figure 7.1.)*

> *Being tired from the energy and the Light He took from Himself, He rested to restore His energy. After He rested, He decided to see how Light enjoyed its existence. He spoke to Light with the voice which seemed far, far away. "This is your Father, Light. How do you like yourself?" Light was totally confused with her father's question. "I do not understand your question, for I do not perceive anything to like or dislike." Her Father repeated a like statement, "You do not perceive anything to like or dislike? Yet you are so brilliant and beautiful. You must be able to see yourself." Light responded, "Father, I see nothing beautiful about myself. In fact, I actually cannot see myself." Father told Light they would speak again at another time, and in His confusion, He withdrew into Himself.*

For a brief time, Father became introspective, while He focused on Light's confusing predicament. This was a new situation for the Almighty, and yet in His wonderful wisdom, He began to understand Light's bewildering situation. For now, He knew that Light's problem was one of contrast, and as long as Light could see no contrast to her illumination, then she could not see it herself. Light's world existed only of Light with the same consistency at all times. There were no variations whatsoever. Light was pure perfection. The Almighty thought for a short time, in His place in time, and knew what to do. The Almighty spoke to Light once again from His place, and said, "Light, I understand your confusion and inability to see yourself. For without contrast in your light, you are without vision, for there is no image of yourself to see in your perfection. Therefore, I will give you your sight. The sight will come in the form of a brother." Light responded quietly, "Father, what is a brother?" And with a warm fatherly tone, the Almighty said, "A brother is one who comes from the same source. Since you come from within me, you are my child. And since your brother will come from within me, he also will be my child, and you will be sister and brother." "Father what will my brother be called?" Father replied, "Light, your brother will be called 'Dark'."

Father then created Light's brother, Dark, and the Dark was a beautiful deep and intense creation. Father was awed by the splendor of His creation, and Dark and Light were equally beautiful in Father's eyes. At that moment that Dark was created, Light could see herself clearly and distinctly. She was taken by her brilliance and beauty and was joyfully pleased. "Oh Father," Light exclaimed, "I can see myself." Light perceived herself in the form of a fairy. Light lifted her arms high above her head and with her palms exposed to the Almighty's love and her head leaned back while taking a deep refreshing breath, experienced her new awareness and the total acceptance of herself and the Almighty's gift of Dark. A feeling of joy permeated her existence. Light asked Dark if he could see how brilliant and beautiful she was and Dark responded in delight, "Oh yes, Light, I can see you and I am glad I am here to be with you."

A moment passed and Light realized she could not see herself before Father created Dark. She humbled herself by dropping her head and wings while she thanked Dark for the beautiful form which he had given her, for without Darkness, Light had no form at all. She was so utterly perfect that you could not see her at all. For without Darkness, Light never really existed except in the eyes of the Almighty. Once

Figure 7.1. "Light," the illumination created. (Artwork by Susan Arnold.)

again she raised her arms and hands upward to the Almighty and said, "Father, I thank you for your wonderful gift of Dark. For together we are actually one. Yes, Father I do realize your wonderful wisdom. The two of us allow each to exist.

Darkness did not understand what she was making such a to-do over. So he spoke to the Almighty, "Father I surely do not see what is so wonderful about giving me to Light." And the Great One responded, "Well, of course not, Darkness, for you have always experienced the contrast between you and your sister, Light. She has always existed for you. So perhaps the only way for you to fully enjoy your own uniqueness is to take away Light for a period of time." And, as He spoke, the Almighty did just that. He took away Light and there was only Dark. And the Darkness was so perfect that Dark could no longer see himself. He had no boundaries and he could, therefore, have no perception of himself. "Father," he spoke loudly with alarm in his voice, "I am lost." "Yes, my son. Now you see the void created when there is only your own perfect existence. And so, as I give you back the gift of your sister, Light, you will understand." Dark spoke at just the next moment, for the Great One had given him back Light. Dark raised his arms up to the Father, smiling warmly with Light pressed against his face, wings and body, giving him a beautiful, intense visual experience of himself and his existence. Darkness did now understand and held his arms up high with his palms exposed to the Almighty. He also took a deep breath and flared his wings in a joyful gesture. Dark spoke, "Thank you, Father for showing me Light and giving me to myself." Darkness said to Light, "Thank you for the wonderful warmth you have given me. I truly can see myself with your existence, and without you, I would be blind and not seem to exist at all." A feeling of gratitude between the two grew until they were consumed within the warmth of their oneness, for together they truly existed. The Almighty spoke, "It pleases me to see you as one and also to see you as individuals. To know that each of you now relies on the other for your completeness." And with His words, an expanding warmth came over them all.

CLIENT'S RECALL OF THERAPY

In Perceptual Adjustment Therapy, we look closely at what exists and look for the positive of each part or state. It is extremely important to see and to have contrast within ourselves and also with others. For without acknowledging the opposite, do we truly exist? Or do we only live in agony and denial?

The following conversation between Jim Holder and Tom is one they both looked forward to for a long period of time. A little history may be in order: A number of years ago, Tom met Jim when he came into treatment and was in a group at that time. The two began to do some work on awareness of the split, or the internal conflict, and looked at the two sides: one being the inactive side, the other being the active side. This was all done in a group situation so that each individual could see the conflict in others and begin to think about his/her own conflict; and also could go through the his/her process, which can become very intense at times. So in the beginning, Tom shared information about his inactive side and the associated positive intents. He also allowed himself to express the positive intents from the active side and actually would step from one side to the other in doing this. He was so congruent in actually showing the two states to Jim, that it was easy for Jim to picture them and to step into one of the states himself, taking on the physiological traits of that state. Tom chose to stay in the state of the inactive, so Jim stepped into the active state. Once Jim took over the physiology that Tom had demonstrated, Jim actually had feelings and thoughts come to him that would come from a person in that state.

Jim knew that Tom's recovery began that day, and he knew that it was a very powerful experience, just by seeing Tom at other times. The two of them never sat down and shared with each other actually what occurred that day. We thought that sharing it here might be an excellent way for people to understand what happened; that is, to actually read it through the eyes and through the feelings of a person who experienced it rather than hearing an individual talk about it from a distance. The reason Jim chose Tom is that he had seen Tom on numerous occasions. In fact, Tom now works in the field. Each time he saw Tom, he saw someone who seemed to be working through a healthy recovery process. For that reason, Jim asked Tom to share with him for purposes of putting some of the information in this book.

Tom now has been clean and sober for five years, but that is only one reason we chose him—the unusual aspect of his case is that he remembers a great deal about how the process started for him, how he first became aware of the parts of himself, and how he began to reconcile and integrate them.

For Tom, the process began during an edu-therapy group when he was in inpatient treatment. The edu-therapy group was a weekly group in which clients participated their first two weeks of treatment. We would alternate each week from first memory work to internal conflict work. The day Tom came in, we were working on the internal conflict. Clients would begin work in these groups, and go back to their regular daily groups and continue to follow up or consolidate these ideas. To have done more in this one group would have drained the power of their daily therapy groups.

> **JIM:**   *The way I was thinking about starting was just to ask what stands out about that day for you and what stands out for me.*

> **TOM:**   *Alright. I had already told myself when I got started with this, I said, "Okay, I'm going to be completely honest. I'm not going to pretend about anything—if it's there, it's there—if it's not, it's not. So that's what I went in with. Basically, I was trying to be real.*

> **JIM:**   *You mean when you volunteered, and were standing up there, you were thinking about it, or before?*

> **TOM:**   *I went in there blank, and when you asked me "How do you act when you're high?" and "What are you aware of?" that was the first time anybody had ever asked me questions like that, or that I had ever thought about it. So I guess that's when I decided to be honest.*

> **JIM:**   *That's my memory, because I remember you pausing for a moment to really think about it. Then I saw you presenting your two different parts congruently, because when you talked, you seemed to go from one side to the other. I could see the difference in your face, and in your mannerisms, your affect, and that's a good indicator that you were being genuine.*

> **TOM:**   *And I think that was me just trying to be real serious about it. I wanted to test what you were doing—find out whether this therapy thing was real or not.*

> **JIM:**   *And you didn't care either way?*

> **TOM:**   *Either way. I wanted to make sure I was not—you know, it's just like when people say I need to get hypnotized. Is that really out there or is it not?*

> **JIM:**   *So we started by asking you to act out the two major parts of yourself—the way you were when you were straight and the way you were when you were high. That was where I could see you were being*

genuine. And I got a clear picture of the physiology of each side. Then I turned around and asked you to choose which you wanted to be.

TOM: *That was the amazing part for me. It's funny—I still tell people today, that after I had portrayed both parts, I don't know why I decided to be the straight part. I think I was in a pretty happy mood. I didn't think I could keep that addict face without chemicals.*

JIM: *After seeing you portray the addict, I had noticed the physiology, and I imitated it in front of you so that you could see what you looked like. And when I did that, you stepped back and looked at me. I broke your state, and when you shifted, I thought to myself, "I got it."*

TOM: *I couldn't believe you had it that well. I mean, I couldn't believe that you could turn around and keep that face. That was when I thought "OK, this is for real." I think from that point, I started trying to snap you out of being my "addict" and prove to you that this therapy didn't work.*

JIM: *Well, what did you feel, when you saw me step in and be your addict? What was the feeling that hit you, when you decided to talk me out of it?*

TOM: *I got real nervous and I think I know why. I'm sure I didn't know it then, but I know today that the addict was the part of me that I used to cope with the world—the adult. Me being me, I was the kid. I think it has to do with authoritative figures. When you turned around looking like my addict, you were all of a sudden an authoritative figure. I can't handle that too well. I think that's where the fear came in.*

JIM: *Just for the record, let me mention what your "addict" looked like—you were pretty scary. You were super-serious, stern, swollen, and proud. Your chest was swollen up, and you looked powerful. That was the physiology that I was imitating.*

TOM: *And like I said, that was the way I tried to cope with the world—my adult.*

JIM: *Do you remember the words I said to you?*

TOM: *Oh, I remember a lot of the words you said to me. I even remember the point that got me enraged. I talk today; when I talk to* *my sponsor I tell him about how the truth pisses me off. Because everything you were saying was pissing me off.*

JIM: *I could see the anger, and I was being provocative. I was saying things like: "Why don't you quit bullshitting these people—you walk around here like you're so cool and you've got it together—and you're just a big phony."*

TOM: *There's so much truth to it though. But at first when you started talking, I was trying to make you stop—I started laughing and giggling because I wanted to divert people's attention and get you away from it. I thought—who are you? You're not me. The one thing that really hit home was when you said "You're like a fast car with no brakes." I was like whoa, you know, nobody talks to me like that. That's when I think that I got real serious. That's when the laugh went away, when you said that. As you kept on talking, you were talking about the only time that I rested was when I was high. And I thought, "This is true about me, but he can't know this." And so I thought part of this was an insult.*

JIM: *Part of it was true and part was an insult.*

TOM: *I mean, all of it was true, but it was an insult that I was doing it to myself. That's where the rage started coming up.*

JIM: *I never felt the rage as a person—in the role, when I was being that part of you, I thought you were angry with that part of yourself, not with me Jim Holder. At that time, I felt like you were enraged too. It was working.*

TOM: *YES!*

JIM: *You see, I've done therapy with people before when they weren't "for real," and then I've done things with people when they were. And in this instance, I thought "Well, this is definitely for real" because I saw you changed too.*

TOM: *And that's why I accepted you as the addict part—as representing that part of me.*

JIM: *Yeah. Oh, you did!*

TOM: *And that's where all that anger and stuff. . . . It wasn't pointed at Jim Holder. I think that at the end, when I felt ashamed I had done everything I could to get you out of the role, you stayed there and went on to talk about it. I still don't understand today how you knew so much. I remember shaking at this point. You know, because you were saying, "What are you gonna do? If you kill me or hurt me, you're going to be hurting yourself." You were egging me on.*

JIM: *Did you say to me, that I'm gonna kill you? I believe you did at one point.*

TOM: *Yeah, I was gonna get rid of you. You said something about, "You can't get rid of me, cause if you get rid of me you're gonna kill yourself." And I think I even said something about that's an option that I have.*

JIM: *Yeah you did.*

TOM: *I was . . . I was there then. And then that's when the tears was coming and I wanted you to stop. I didn't want to play no more. It's like, okay, now I know for sure that this thing works. That's what I was thinking.*

JIM: *Okay.*

TOM: *And I wanted to get out of it. I remember then trying to figure out a way to get out because I was . . . tears was coming up. I didn't want them people to see me cry.*

JIM: *Okay.*

TOM: *And from the rage, all of a sudden it disappeared and just total hurt was there. I remember saying, you know . . . "you get out of being who you are and come back to being Jim Holder."*

JIM: *Yeah. And I said okay. At that moment, I stepped out I think.*

TOM: *I think so, and that's when I remember leaving.*

JIM: *You walked around the room. In fact, you left the circle of chairs, you walked in a circle and walked around and came back and got back in the group and sat over, away from me. You sat over in the* *corner, not the corner, but across from me.   Next to the door, as a matter of fact.*

TOM: *After a while you came around there, though.*

JIM: *I walked over to you?*

TOM: *You walked over there and kind of rubbed my shoulder. And that's what made it okay to come back. You know, cause I was . . . all the information I was getting just totally overwhelmed me.*

JIM: *Remember when you said you wondered how I could know the stuff I knew? I've got a lot of experience with this stuff, but the most important information is what you gave to me. When I watched you be that active part of you, when I watched you be that addict, I noticed every little thing I could. Physically, I looked at how your shoulders were, how your head was, the look on your face, everything about you, the tone of your voice. Then I assumed that physiology and those words just started coming. It was like I had that knowledge. When I took on that stance that you were in, that physiology, those words just started coming real easy. On one hand it was me and on the other hand, it wasn't me either. I didn't know what was coming next. You would say something and the words would come automatically. I was aware of what was happening, and sometimes I would think, "This is working, I'm right on target." So I just kept letting it happen because I knew that whatever was happening was real and it was true.*

TOM: *That's right. I think there's even a point in time I tried to get silent and quit ahead of time, but you know, that one thing about the fast car just . . .*

JIM: *No brakes . . .*

JIM: *Okay, so when I look at it now, I'm wondering how you did come together within yourself. How do you deal with yourself—with the part that was inactive that didn't want to use anymore and the part that at one time was your "adult," as you say, to show to people? How did you integrate those parts?*

TOM: *I think the biggest thing was to have to stay there, in treatment, after all that was done. For about two days, I didn't exactly want to be "happy, joyous, and free." I didn't want to be a people pleaser.*

JIM: *So you began to break out of your role in life at that point?*

TOM: *Yeah. I examined all that and today what I tell myself, I'll say, "Okay. My biggest thing now is not to try and be a big people pleaser. My biggest thing today is to have a program. We've got this thing called HALT—you know, hungry, angry, lonely, tired.*

JIM: *Right. So there are two main ideas: one, that you've learned to put yourself first and take care of yourself, and two, that you've given yourself some brakes by having a program.*

TOM: *I was writing some stuff and, well, this is a little bit of my Third Step where I was getting with God and I said, "Okay, when I'm doing too much, you know, let me get a headache." That's a warning signal for me to slow down.*

JIM: *For you. Okay.*

TOM: *You know the greatest thing to have keyed in on, I tell people today the words "Slowly Committing Suicide." I do know that at a point, if I'd have kept using, I would have been so pissed off with the Active part that he would have probably tried to commit suicide.*

JIM: *It could have happened.*

TOM: *Yeah, in order to get rid of him, you know. But I never thought of that consciously.*

JIM: *Okay. So, really what happened then, you said for the next couple of days, you didn't try to please other people. You got real serious. So, basically, you took on the Active part, the part that liked to use, then. Are you saying that you allowed that part of yourself to come alive in a new way?*

TOM: *I couldn't understand it at the time, when you said, "Now instead of using crack, just slow down." A lot of my stuff, when I used, especially when I drank, it was to say something to somebody that I couldn't say when I wasn't high.*

JIM: *To be more than a people pleaser. So one of your positive intents for using was be more confident and outspoken.*

TOM: *Yeah. So when I was high, I thought I was okay. Now, if somebody comes up or something's going on, I'm going to have to say what I think or what I feel. I still do a process system where I write about things. I say, "Okay, how's this affecting me?" That's kind of like what I do.*

JIM: *So you do a check with all of yourself, and it's a way to just slow yourself down in a healthy way.*

TOM: *Uh-huh. Well, it's going ahead and doing what the old active side, my using side, my adult, knows needs to be done.*

JIM: *So instead of a conflict, you have more of a dialogue with yourself and just work it out and go ahead and do what you need to do.*

TOM: *Finally it will come to a point where I say, "Okay, either this is going to happen or this is going to happen."*

JIM: *Okay.*

TOM: *Yeah, that's what. And I do it more at work than anywhere else.*

JIM: *So the active part says, "Okay, you need to take action now because it's gone too far."*

TOM: *Yeah. It's time to do something. Like I say, I can just feel it coming on. At first I'll try and get away from everybody or I try to slow down and say, "Okay, what's going on?" I don't actually say that out loud, but that's what I'm thinking. You know, what's going on? What is being done that is pissing us off? You know and once I figure that out it's like well you gotta do something about it. You know, cause if not, it's gonna fester, fester and get back to that breaking point.*

JIM: *Just now, you just said "pissing us off." You used those words and I understand them. In reality, though, do you really see yourself as one?*

TOM: *Yes.*

JIM: *That's what I thought. So you use that just messing with yourself a little bit and say, "Okay, get it together."*

TOM: *Well see, that's what I'm saying; that's when the headache starts coming in.*

JIM: *So the final signal then, is the headache?*

TOM: *Yeah.*

JIM: *Okay, have you reached this breaking point with a headache and had a strong desire to use?*

TOM: *Yeah, but only once in my recovery. The strong desire to use came afterwards and it had something to do with dealing with the president of the company where I work that I thought I was being . . . I don't know, misused, and I was trying to say, "It will be alright." I got the headache, but I said it wasn't because of that. It was because I didn't have plenty of rest. So, you know . . .*

JIM: *You ignored the headache?*

TOM: *Yeah. I ignored the headache and went home and then got some rest, but that wasn't the problem. Then the next day, coming from work, just this strong desire to use came. I mean, it felt like I had just tasted some crack, and I was like, "Wow! Where did that come from?" I said, "Okay, when you get home, it's time to do some work." I just got out the pen and started writing, and what was festering up was the stuff that was going on at work. Then the next day, I came back and told them, "Hey, we need to talk."*

JIM: *Okay.*

TOM: *It went up the chain of command. I talked to everybody I needed to talk to.*

JIM: *Great. Okay, now the other part—how did you give yourself this signal of a headache? When I work with people I can give their active side a signal to use, but if they're not paying attention, and they don't deal with it at the time, the active side will go on to suggest that they use. That's really just a sign that they haven't been paying attention to the signal. Still, I don't remember doing that with you, and you got a signal of a headache. So, how did you come up with that?*

TOM: *Actually, I knew something had to happen that would help me.*

JIM: *Did you consciously think about giving yourself a headache?*

TOM: *I did that in a third step when I was talking to God and getting a conscious contact with Him. And I said, "Well, okay, you know, I need a signal, God. You know, I've been waiting on you to come down here and talk to me and have it out." But instead, He gives me a headache.*

JIM: *Okay.*

TOM: *Now my number one thing when I get a headache is to just stop. I don't know what's going on, but I know something's going wrong.*

JIM: *Okay. Then that's your time when you write. When you get with yourself, sit yourself down, and start writing.*

TOM: *Yeah. I write. I just get back and analyze what's going on.*

JIM: *You go inward.*

TOM: *Yeah. I get away and just sit down when something's wrong.*

JIM: *That's neat. We didn't finish the integration process. We started it. And what's neat is you just told me how you begin to finish it. You finished it with God. And you talked to God and thought about what you need and that was the way you finished the integration process.*

TOM: *Yeah, but you see, you helped because after that one particular time in group, every time I tried to get back with you, you would send me to my regular daily group.*

JIM: *Right.*

TOM: *I would try to talk to you again and you would say, "You need to take that up with your group." Until then, I didn't have any confidence in the group.*

JIM: *Okay.*

TOM: *And then I began to see that the group works.*

JIM: *And I didn't want you to become dependent on me.*

TOM: *Right.*

JIM: *So I kept . . .*

TOM: *. . . brushing me off. Every time I saw you, you kept brushing me off. All of a sudden I thought, I know what I need. You know? And I just started doing it myself, so to speak. But getting help from other people indirectly and that's when some of the outside people in NA started coming into my life and I was sharing with them some of the stuff that happened. That's when I began to find my place.*

JIM: *That's wonderful. How else has it affected your spirituality?*

TOM: *Cause I . . . it's uh . . . the thing with me is that growing up, I always remember everybody telling me about God and what God meant, but only other people's perception of Him. So, there came a point in time where I fired them. I fired my mom, my dad, my grandmother, anybody that told me anything about God. You got to cross your legs and got to do this and do that. I just fired them all. And I just got on my knees one night and I talked to Him and said, "Look, you know, I need someone that's gonna be loving and caring. I'm gonna make mistakes. I definitely need somebody who can forgive me." I said, "If you can do that for me, we're in business."*

JIM: *I think this is when you really totally integrated yourself. At that moment, you were one with yourself. The moment you were one with yourself, you were also one with God, and the circle was complete.*

Chapter 8

THE DEPENDENT FAMILY SYSTEM: OPPOSITE SIDES OF THE SAME COIN

The apparent helplessness seated in the dependent person's internal conflict gives rise to the "rescuing" role of the codependent. This is the basis for the dependent family system.

A first thing to consider when looking at the family is to explore how each individual in the family contributes to the family balance. We all look for a place to belong in life. We are social creatures searching for a way to fit into society. Our first learning/practice arena, then, is our own family.

The family itself is striving to have balance within. A healthier family is able to find balance and maintain a supportive system in which a great deal of encouragement is evident. The encouragement supports each individual in having flexibility in their personality and a positive place in the family. Encouraged individuals have balance within the family, and family members enjoy (for the most part) the flexible roles they choose. The way they find themselves relating to the family is rewarding to each individual, giving them the ability to show "both sides of the coin." For example, instead of being locked in a role where a child is "the shy one," he/she would have the opportunity (and be encouraged) to exhibit both outgoing and reserved characteristics. So each member in the family will find ways to encourage other members in the family in their own multiphase existence.

Once a family has established a balance, it will fight extremely hard to maintain the balance. A healthy family will fight just as hard as an unhealthy family to maintain balance and the status quo. One difference you might see in a healthier family is that siblings may be more similar than different. For example, you may see a family where doing well in school or positively exhibiting intelligence is important for all the children. Even though they may pick different ways to express it, or they may have a few subjects that they enjoy just a little more, the fact that each of the siblings share this family value is a reflection of a healthy environment. In an unhealthy family, you would see the siblings in more competitive roles—one being the good child and one the bad child; one making very high grades and one making very poor grades.

In explaining how this takes place, let us look at a family and the siblings in a family as young children. First of all, when a child comes into the world, he/she has a strong desire to find his/her place of recognition in the family. The parents have already established some balance in their relationship. So as the children are born, they strive for balance also. The easiest way to see this is in the good child/bad child scenario. In families where you see an angel, you may also see a child who people consider a menace—always getting in some kind of trouble. So this little snap-a-roo is just as good at rebellion and mischief as the angel is at being perfect and in total harmony with mom and dad. Look at our biblical "first family." Adam and Eve had two sons, Cain and Abel, who demonstrated this balance. Cain was just as bad as Abel was good. So the Judeo-Christian heritage starts off talking about family balance and how children will compete with each other. Some children will compete in a healthy way and strive to find a positive place. Other children will compete in a more negative light, and one of the children will find it pays off to be the best at being bad, as Cain did. The metaphor of family balance and individuals seeking roles within the family goes all the way back to the beginning of recorded history.

It is vitally important to understand sibling rivalry and how children find their place in relation to each other. For instance, it may happen that one child finds a place in being shy; the other will very likely discover that it is in his/her interest to exhibit characteristics that are more engaging of others. In this case, each child gives up a part of himself/herself. Each chooses to no longer exhibit certain behaviors because these behaviors are contradictory to his/her perceived place in the family—these behaviors are no longer beneficial. Adult family members overtly and covertly encourage this role-hardening when they begin to limit their perceptions of their children, labelling them and fixing their roles. In fact, this is not limited to families with siblings—families with just one child tend to encourage only certain aspects of that child's potential, forcing him/her into a role.

Imagine an addicted family where one child is physically healthy and the other sickly. The sickly child grows into adulthood and addicts himself/herself to alcohol. Within this addicted sibling rages what appears to be the internal conflict we have talked so much about in this book—the conflict over whether or not to use chemicals. Now consider a paradoxical shift in understanding conflict: "Conflict is a carefully orchestrated dance—one step forward, one step backward—the final result being to consistently remain at dead center." While one perceives oneself in the throes of an internal addictive conflict, unable to move through an impasse, the reality is that these unproductive thoughts, feelings, and behaviors are created because of an unwillingness/inability to move in the direction of a productive outcome.

If the problem is solved and the impasse breached, the chosen role in the family must be forsaken, and to forsake the role is perceived as both suicide and betrayal. That is, at a perceptual level, in killing the fantasy role, the client feels as though he is killing himself and his family. In reality, he only is being asked to experience life in the here and now with the use of an adjusted perceptual filter.

In this light, we can see that "hitting bottom" is the same thing as reaching what Gestalt therapists would call a ***death state***. The impasse is perceived in its entirety, and the facade of both role and conflict is no longer productive or acceptable to the participant. Exposed in this way, naked for the first time before himself/herself, the true person emerges into the world experiencing true feelings of anger, joy, and grief.

Do you see the paradoxical shift here? *The conflict is purposeful.* The conflict is a process structured by the individual to support his/her belief system— the belief system that gave birth to his/her chosen role. The belief system (and ultimately the role and the conflict) was perceived as necessary by the child in order to arrive at a specific goal in relating to the family. Adlerian psychologists call these the "misguided goals" and identify them as attention, power, revenge, and inadequacy.

Let us consider our example of the healthy child/sickly child again. I once had a patient in treatment who, after making his first phone call to his family, seemed so excited that he stopped me in my tracks reporting the experience.

"Hey! Guess where I am?" he said to his parents, "I'm in the hospital, and I want you to come bring me some things."

He sounded like a kid at Christmas time, and I was struck speechless.

Later in treatment, he described an early memory that metaphorically fit with his present situation and the phone call. In the memory, he was five or six years old, and was in the hospital. The part that stuck out for him was all the attention and gifts he received while there. His feelings were of excitement and unconditional acceptance.

His alcoholism, then, became the means for attaining this goal (attention and acceptance) again. As therapists, what we can do is enlighten the patient and his family regarding ways to develop and support positive behaviors that will result in attention and acceptance. At the same time, we should address the positive intents behind his family members' enabling and pampering.

Let us say that in this case the client's mother and sister had been the ones who usually visited him in the hospital and brought him things. They did so with positive intentions. They believed that he was victimized by his poor health—that he never had the opportunity to achieve in the same way as his siblings. Their positive intents were to let him know that they cared about him, and in so doing, to gain positive feelings of self-esteem for themselves.

Hopefully, you can already see the setup here. They became dependent upon his sickness to feel good about themselves, just as he became dependent upon their attention to feel good temporarily. Unfortunately, this cycle is ultimately self-defeating, because each time it occurs, his underlying sense of self-worth is eroded just a bit. This causes negative feelings that will vanish while under the influence of alcohol. With chemicals, he learns to achieve a sense of short-lived empowerment and a desire to abuse again.

In treatment, we need to remember that just because the internal conflict is a self-created fantasy, that does not mean that we can not use it to good advantage. The internal conflict is a key tool in assisting the client to acknowledge the impasse and break through it, which is the start of the journey up.

So this balancing of roles will go on with family members all the way through their lives. When siblings reach adult life, you will see them struggle to maintain it. If one of the adult children begins to change, then that will throw the family out of balance, and someone will strive to rebalance the family.

For example, a sibling may begin to make a change in life, and another family member will resist it or change themselves to reapproximate balance. Perhaps one was a fear-based child who later became a drinker. During treatment, he/she begins to develop new confidence. At this point, you may see another member of the same dependent family start to abuse alcohol or find ways of discouraging that individual's sobriety. Either of these two subconscious strategies would rebalance the family in some fashion. Neither is deliberate. The thing to remember is that they are out of balance and that they strive to keep these things in balance, or at least to maintain the status quo.

In maintaining the status quo, we might say that dependent families develop a mythology—that is, a pattern emerges for the interrelationship of their roles that helps them to rationalize their behavior. For example, a family may establish a pattern of crisis and dependency for generations that results in a particular event like divorce or suicide. While all of the family members regard the event as tragic, they simultaneously support the unproductive roles that give rise to it. In this way, you will often see a repeated story in family histories.

One of my clients arrived in treatment in the midst of a divorce. After looking at his family history, we discovered that he was living out the same pattern of roles and relationships that his father had before him. His father even had divorced his mother at the same age—47.

As therapists, we can recognize that anytime change is introduced, a family's mythology is challenged. Without counseling, at least one of the family members will attempt to reestablish the pattern of the family's mythology. By making families aware of their own mythologies, however, the counselor offers them the opportunity to see beyond their present roles and to choose a new, more productive pattern for themselves.

So when you think about families in this way, you can see the importance of having families come in for treatment when there is alcohol and drug dependency. Any program that does not bring families in for treatment is making a terrible mistake, because when the individual goes home and is in the recovery process, something has got to give in the family. If you have each person in the family in therapy, then you can see each person begin to shift and find more healthy ways to find the family's balance.

I recently was talking to an individual who had gone through inpatient treatment a few years ago. When we stood in the yard and talked, he shared with me that he had divorced his wife. One of the things that he stated was that she told him she actually liked him better drinking than being sober. What happened was when he returned from treatment, he became more assertive. He began to take more responsibility for the first time. He became a better parent for his children. He took more responsibility in the family, and he asked to have more of a say in what happened with the family. He wanted to talk over financial decisions with his spouse before they took action. This was such a disruptive event for his wife, who had full control for years during his drinking, that she would not relinquish control and no longer wanted to be married to him. So they divorced. He is remarried at this time and has a wife who enjoys a responsible husband who works together with her in conducting family business and family rituals. If we would have had more time that afternoon, I would have loved to find out if any of his siblings were having difficulties in life or with their parents since he was doing so well in his life.

In working with both young children and adult children who have an established place in the family, a clear cue that you are beginning to make progress is that the good child, or the so-called good child, will begin to misbehave. The reason this happens is that the other sibling will attempt to bring things back into balance. Since he/she has been in balance with his/her sibling, he/she is the first to know that something is happening. It is as if the two are connected, and as soon as one begins to change, the other begins to change. It may be before the therapist or the mother or father would actually see it. So when you are working with a family, one of the first indicators of progress may be that another sibling will begin to act out or abuse something. That is a time to share with the parents that it is okay—that what is happening is that the two children are attempting to reestablish their places in the family and are striving to maintain the old unhealthy pattern. So what is happening is to be expected. At this point, it is exceedingly important for parents and other family members to remain consistent in their new behaviors, and soon both kids will begin to behave. I have actually worked with families that came to me after having left another counselor because the good child began to get in trouble. They said that things were not getting better, they were getting worse. Then they quit. Isn't it amazing how it works? The sibling, just like a spouse of an alcoholic, works to reestablish the status quo.

In Figure 8.1, family "C" is essentially a copy of family "A" and family "B." This is because the father and mother in "C" were each seeking to establish balance for themselves.

Though this is somewhat oversimplified, you will see startling patterns of generational replication in families. Some are simple repetitions of relationships, some are marvelously complex arrangements of support systems, but all have generational balance as their goal.

There are two major principles we want to keep in mind with this understanding: First, things with the dependent or abusing family member will have a tendency to get worse. For example, if you are a child who has found your place by abusing chemicals, and all of a sudden your parents are acting a new

GENERATIONAL BALANCE IN ADDICTED FAMILY SYSTEMS

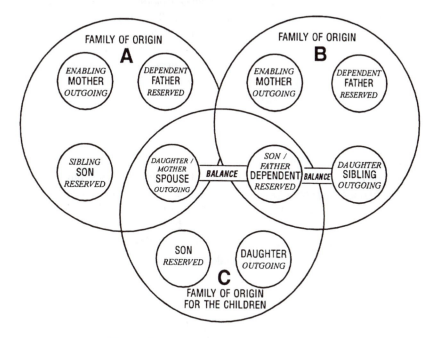

Figure 8.1. Generational balance diagram.

way in which you are not getting the same notoriety for your dependency, you will try even harder to regain the attention and maintain the balance. If the dependent family member gets a little worse, that is okay. You can expect that. Second, the clincher will be when the balancing family member begins to behave differently. At that point, you know you truly are having success with your therapy. In family therapy, you have not made progress until someone begins to act out or to make a shift in some way. At that point, you know that you are having success in your treatment because the family is, for the first time in years, out of balance.

So once again, we have a paradox. In order to help people get in balance with themselves, we must knock the family out of balance so that everyone can begin to experience their true selves and how to live in the here and now. Once you know a few of these simple rules, family therapy becomes wonderfully exciting because you can begin to read between the lines. You can begin to see when you are having a positive impact.

The way to end the crisis within an addicted family is to set up controlled crisis in order to bring about new health and stability for each member of the family. Fire fighters use a similar technique. Fire fighters quite often will set up a controlled burn or backfire to stop a raging forest fire. That is, they will set a fire to stop a fire. It is basically the same concept that we are talking about. In order to help this out-of-control family find some stability in their lives, we as professionals may set up some control situations.

A control situation can be as simple as this example: Let us say that even after several months of sobriety, therapy, and family change, a husband and wife are continuing to argue with each other every day. A control situation can be implemented by asking them to record the basic pattern of their conflict (usually this is well known to them, and has 3 to 7 basic parts). Have them set aside a specific time each day to go through the process for 5 to 10 minutes; that is, give them permission to argue regularly, and ask them to follow the pattern they have established. By the third or fourth day, most couples reach a point where their conflict will never again be the same and often ends almost completely.

Remember, our goal is to facilitate health in the family that may not have been there for generations. We view addictions as a family disease not just an individual disease. The recovering individual has a much better chance of recovery once the family is brought into therapy. If we as therapists do not see the importance of bringing the family in, then we are ignoring the addicted system, and out of ignoring comes ignorance.

THE FAMILY SESSION

I. INTERVENTION STAGE (First phone call)

Get the whole family in for counseling.
In couples counseling, see both partners every session.
In parenting counseling, see both parents and all children.
In dependency counseling, bring in as many generations as possible.
Setting up the first appointment is crucial to success.
There are times when education on the importance of family involvement
   is necessary.

There are times when an awareness of the codependent's feelings is the easiest way to bring a codependent in for counseling.
Use their desire to help as a means to assure their attendance.

II. SESSION PREPARATION STAGE

Set up office chairs as close together as possible.
Have any necessary paperwork at hand.
Observe how the family members seat themselves in your office. Look for sub-groups. Are the parents together, or are the kids in between them?

III. SOCIAL STAGE

Introduce yourself to the family.
Go over any necessary rules or rights—confidentiality, for example.
Explain the room/video equipment, etc.
Join with the family by developing rapport.
Speak to each member to get a response, and find out a few things about each.
Be respectful of any cultural issues before you.
Deal with missing members.
Respect generational boundaries the family may have.
Remember: you are observing and establishing rapport.

IV. GOAL IDENTIFICATION/TREATMENT STAGE

Address each member to acquire the positive outcome each wishes for the session.
Address each member to acquire the positive outcome each wishes for the entire counseling process.
Educate the family on Positive Intents and how this will be used to accomplish their goals.
Determine which goal the family wishes to begin with first.
Allow appropriate interaction between family members.
Allow parent to handle any interruptions by the children.
Encourage interaction among family members.
Begin to pace and lead as necessary (See Chapter 12).
Set up situations to encourage interaction when necessary.
Use educational assignments to break through family denial and develop self-awareness.

Do integration work with family members where appropriate (See Chapter 12).

Do assessments with early memories on both dependents and codependents (See Chapter 12).

V. CLOSING STAGE

Restate family goals before closing.

Set appointments for next session.

Confirm contract for three sessions with each family member. Where more than three sessions are needed, contract again.

WORKSHOP EXCERPTS

Q: *"So you're saying a person is always working to reestablish the old balance they had in the family?"*

A: *Yes. When we marry and have our own children, we reestablish the balance and work as hard as we can to have a familiar family system around us. When we work in our workplace, we work for the same balance so we may find individuals who we don't work very well with, just as we did our siblings. In our marriages we may find a spouse who's very similar to one of the siblings who had the most impact on us, or who we found our balance with on the most significant level.*

Q: *If we get in balance with a given role, we get out of balance with ourselves.*

A: *Yes, the moment we choose the limitation of a role, we become out of balance with ourselves. Specifically, we're talking about the fact that we give up a part of what we are, if we discard options with our personalities.*

Q: *What about individual differences? When people come into the world, they have their own little personality. How much of that is finding balance, and how much of that is being an individual with your own personality characteristics?*

A: *We have a difference in bias here. I believe we come into the world or a family and develop our personalities through our percep-*

tions and the decisions we make around our perceptions. Remember, perceptions include all your senses. This involves genetics, in that the activity of our senses can be determined genetically. One of the obvious reasons for my bias is from observing how often firstborns seem to be similar and how often second-borns seem to be similar. Firstborns have a tendency to be a little more goal-directed, serious minded, in the way they see the world. They may make high grades in many cases. Second-borns (or the babies) may be more playful, carefree action-takers, somewhat the opposite of the firstborn.

Sharon Wegschieder-Cruse (1989) also talked about this when she discussed the roles of kids in a dependent family. The "hero" is most often the firstborn. They have a tendency to excel in what they do. They are the ones who tend to go to the best college. They will have a tendency to make the best grades or be the captain of the football team. The "scapegoat," who quite often would be (in a family of two) the second-born, would be somewhat more rebellious and would have a tendency to use chemicals much earlier in life. The scapegoat's grades might not be as important to them. The "lost child" quite often would be the third-born in a family of four. This lost child may be one who stays to himself/herself more often, does not have quite as many friends, and may possibly be more of a bookworm. Quite often the family worries about him/her in the early years because he/she is somewhat of a loner. The "clown" or "mascot" is usually the baby in the family who deals with stress in life through humor. The mascot plays his/her way through life. The mascot is also extremely good at getting the family involved with himself/herself and bringing others into his/her service. The fact that these characteristics (and many others) can be seen in so many families by the place the child is born in the family shows that the personality developed in relationship to how a person perceives himself/herself in a family.

Q: *For instance, what about the next generation? A lot of our families that go through recovery are changing for more democratic families. What happens to the kids?*

A: *Hopefully, we'll see a less dependent, more encouraged group of kids. Instead of being enmeshed with their parents, they'll be more in tune with themselves, their relationship to a higher power, and the interrelationships of the family. They will realize that they are not in this world to live up to anyone else's expectations and instead will decide upon, and live up to, their own. Honest communication can* *permeate future generations and become a culturally accepted way of life.*

Q: *So balance in families is interactive—someone does something and it pulls others in the same way?*

A: *It is just like a mobile; if one portion of a mobile experiences stress, it begins to move, and every other part of the mobile begins to move in response. The movement is not necessarily in the same direction, though. As one individual get healthier, another may begin acting out in negative ways to keep the family in balance. With family counseling, however, each individual's private logic can be discovered, opening new doors for healthy alternatives. The family system's private logic or mythology will also come into view, assisting the family in moving through the transformation as a unit.*

Q: *Does that have a lot to do with age?*

A: *In some ways it does, and in some ways it doesn't. If you're speaking about two siblings, one may have been basically the good kid, let's say, and the other the bad kid. The bad kid begins to make changes in his/her life and be more productive and to find more positive ways to behave. At that point, you would see this supposedly good kid make a shift and begin to act out in most cases. When you have knowledge of this move and you begin to keep working in the same positive ways and relating to family and having the family relate to each other in the same positive ways, both siblings will begin to realize balance in a more positive place. Age doesn't play such an important role there. You could see the same children go through a change like this whether they were five years old or 35 years old. For example, a parent becomes addicted and has given up personal responsibility. He/she begins to move backwards in age-maturity. He/she becomes younger as the addiction becomes more pronounced. As that parent becomes younger, one of the children may leap forward and become older—more mature—and actually develop a rivalry with the parent. So you may have a father and a son beginning to be rivals, switching places because of the addiction.*

Q: *If you see five or six years difference in age, you wouldn't see the sibling rivalry as much?*

A: *Yes, if they're within four years of each other, you see it quite often; less often as the age difference increases.*

Q: *Jim, what about only children?*

A: *Most often only children have a tendency to be more adult-like. Also, they will pick up a number of characteristics of addictive families. They may move in and out of more than one role. Also, in dealing with an only child of an addictive family, you may see the child switch places with the abuser. As I mentioned before, when the abuser begins to become younger in age as far as taking personal responsibility, and becomes more irresponsible and childish, the only child could become much more adult-like and begin to take over responsibilities of this adult. So in many cases, there will be a great deal of turmoil with that child when the parent begins to sober up, especially if the child wasn't involved in family therapy with the parents. Let me rephrase that: you would see it either way, whether he/she was in therapy or not; however, if the child was in therapy, this would give the family the opportunity to give each other support and encouragement for being all each could be, to accept all their options in life.*

Q: *Are personalities acquired to get attention?*

A: *Not exactly. Personalities come from our desire to find our place in our family. We begin to use those personality characteristics that seem to work the best for us. Or, at least in our perception, they work the best for us in terms of how we see the world.*

Q: *So, you're saying I acquired this because of what I saw going on in the family?*

A: *To be more precise, I am saying that your personal decisions about what you saw, heard, and felt in your family environment are based on your perceptions. The trouble we run into is that when these decisions were made, you were only three or four years old and did not have a lot of prior experience to work with. Children often make grandiose global decisions about what they see, or should I say, perceive.*

Q: *I was going to say, how was I so smart to make those decisions, when I couldn't even tie my own shoe?*

A: *I didn't say they were healthy or wise decisions. Seriously, though, part of this centers around this mistaken belief we develop. Another part is that we decide what seems to work best for us. One child may choose to tie his/her shoe at eight. The other at five. The five-year-old* *may find himself/herself being more independent, while the eight-year-old may find himself/herself developing a wonderful ability to bring other individuals into his/her service, most often Mom or Dad or an older sibling, believing, "I am only okay when others are in my service." This belief will cause difficulties in many situations.*

Q: *So, you're saying this personality is more a survival skill than a cognitive process.*

A: *No, I don't believe it's a survival skill. I believe it's a cognitive process. I think we decide what works the best for us according to our belief system. So those personality traits that seem to be the most productive for us are the ones we'll have a tendency to use again. "Productive" might be defined as reinforcing our belief system or family mythology. The child does what works for him or her. If the child has begun to find his/her place through attention seeking behavior, the child will continue to do that, until that no longer works for him/her. It is very similar to the ways children have the ability to learn languages at such a young age. When I was a young teenager, my family lived in Mexico. There was a next door neighbor who had daughters who were probably seven years old. The two seven-year-olds seemed to pick up Spanish much quicker than I did. In language, a child under 11 years old seems to learn more quickly. This is true prior to adolescence. The two seven-year-olds learned to speak the language by finding what works and reproducing it. An adolescent or adult has higher cognitive abilities, even abstract thought, and he/she wishes to understand the meaning of a word and plug it in. This cognitive process makes learning slower.*

Q: *You mentioned that as children we choose a role, and as we take on this role, this throws us out of balance with ourselves. So then, you're saying it's bad to accept a role in the family or to have a role; and if that's so, how do your avoid it?*

A: *I don't believe it's always bad to pick a role in our family. I'm basically saying that's what we do as individuals. Now I am saying the role that we choose causes us to have a greater or lessor degree of discomfort or struggle in our lives. Instead of the word bad, let's say that by choosing the role we give ourselves fewer options or choices. Let's pretend for a moment that life is like building a house. As we come together to build this house, we choose to become proficient with those tools that our primary sibling is not proficient with. So if there*

*were two of us, basically, each of us may have proficiency with half
the given tools. This may work well as we're going through life with
our sibling, because together, we're able to accomplish a lot for the
family—we can build a house. However, if that sibling is no longer
with us, building a house becomes quite a chore. Because some of the
tools that are needed, and some of the skills that are needed in using
these tools, may not seem to be available to us; we'll have to learn to
develop these skills or give up on building a house. Or find someone to
share our life with who has our missing skills.*

Q: *My father has a sister close to him in age. My aunt talked earlier,
and he walked earlier. He was three years old before he ever talked.
He said a whole sentence when he finally decided to talk: "Pass the
mashed potatoes, please." This meant that he could talk, but the family
didn't think he was supposed to talk.*

A: *I bet he also had an additional reason not to talk. That was that
he had others who would talk for him. There more than likely was
someone in the family who was in his service, who was his spokesper-
son.*

Q: *He had no need to.*

A: *That's right. His silence was working for him.*

Q: *Balance in the family—isn't that related to how healthily a family
is functioning?*

A: *A healthy family allows you to have all your parts; you don't
have to be a good girl or a bad girl. In healthier families, there will be
a blend of different personality traits. You may see where both children
happen to be extremely sociable; or in a family with four children, it
may be that all the children are sociable and have a group of friends.
All the children may be considered intelligent but be allowed to make
mistakes. You also may find in healthier families that the children will
be different from one another—but different as a function of free choice,
not different as a reaction to other siblings or misperceptions. So yes,
in a healthier family, you'll see a balance where the children have
more of a pleasant variety and a blend of possibilities. There would be
a greater chance of the individual being more pleased with himself/
herself, and with the family at the same time. Which is the goal we're
striving for in the long run.*

Q: *I come from a family where she is as good as she is bad. They had a tendency to want my sister to be the bad one and me to be the good one. Any time my sister or I did the opposite, the family just freaked. My sister and I knew we were both as good as we were bad. So we banded together and we didn't polarize ourselves.*

Q: *What is codependency?*

OTHER PARTICIPANTS: *I've never found a person who isn't codependent.*

A: *Well, you'll have a hard time not finding one in this room.* (Laughter.) *Basically, the reason I said that is all counselors have a tendency to feel responsible for their clients, to take responsibility for their clients. And I'm sure most of the people in this room come from dependent families.*

Q: Still, I'm not sure what you mean by codependency.

A: *Okay. Codependency means playing a role in the addiction process, contributing to it, feeding off of it. The easiest way to identify it is as a preoccupation with substances and the opinions of other people. There are several very typical results from this—rigidity in attitude and behavior, a low sense of self-esteem, and of course, chemical addiction itself and other compulsive behaviors.*

Codependents are usually people who grow up in dependent families. They exhibit many irresponsible behaviors, such as denial of feelings and a preoccupation with the opinions of others.

Codependents are individuals dependent on the actions of others. In addictions, a codependent person can always escape into the dependency of others, thereby avoiding looking at himself/herself and simultaneously validating his/her misperception of himself/herself. Codependents act in ways that support or enable the addicted person to continue in his/her role. Codependency usually moves on to some form of dependency or compulsive behavior (e.g. alcoholism, drug addiction, overeating, workaholism, gambling, sex addiction, etc.).

Untreated children raised in a dependent family seem to have two obvious choices: one is to become dependent and the other is to remain codependent. Understand that we reestablish our family of origin. If

THE EVOLUTIONARY PROCESS
OF DEPENDENCY

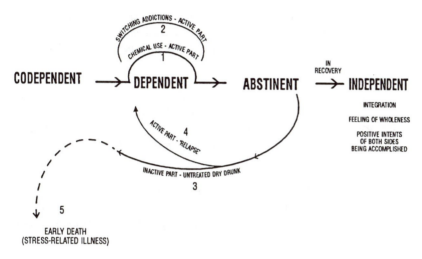

Figure 8.2. The evolutionary process of dependency.

children come from a dependent family made up of one dependent parent and one codependent parent whose dependency is an obsession with the dependent, then the children may see only these two options from which to choose. The sex of the dependent/codependent in the family of origin will influence which sex will most likely become dependent and which will remain codependent.

Those reared in an addicted (codependent) family most often develop a rigid role or mythology. This codependent role becomes the inactive part once substances (alcohol, drugs, food, etc.) bring about desired changes in an individual, releasing them from the rigidity and pain they have been suffering. Or a person may choose the alternate route of focussing all his/her attention on another, so that the person no longer has to feel his/her own pain or discomfort. This person typically will be a spouse or other family member. A dependency evolves out of this repeated use of something or someone to relieve pain, and the active part comes into being.

Once both parts have been established, the perceived internal conflict begins to rage. The dependent user is in conflict over whether to use or not; the codependent is in conflict over whether to be responsible for the dependent or not.

Two choices stemming from the active part are to continue to use despite adverse consequences or to switch addictions to another chemical or person. Both choices leave the active part in control and the inactive part suppressed.

To abstain without treatment brings the inactive part back into power. Two choices stem from this: remain abstinent for a period of time on a dry drunk until rigidity leads to frustration and then relapse giving the active part control again; or continue in a rigid lifestyle into (usually) early stress-related death.

Neither the dependent nor the codependent person has truly beneficial options as long as he/she operates entirely out of either the active or the inactive part. A recovery process requires the integration of these parts and the choice to live life in the here and now.

Genograms

Genograms can be most helpful in understanding codependency and balance in a family. With regard to balancing, you may see examples such as the following:

1.   *The oldest in each generation being dependent.*
2.   *All boys being dependent.*
3.   *All females being codependent.*
4.   *The youngest being dependent.*
5.   *All females having eating disorders.*

The possibilities go on and on. The point is to look for patterns within the system, intergenerationally.

The family tree/genogram may show similar characteristics in both families, mother's and father's. Having similar characteristics keeps an addictive balance. For example, a husband says women on his side of the family are assertive and controlling. The wife says that women on her side of the family take charge. So by marrying each other, they expand the family systems, yet the role of women taking charge or being assertive stays intact.

There is enough information on genograms to write a separate book. My suggestion is to begin to use them with your clients, both dependents and codependents. A genogram is a wonderful tool for breaking through denial, and it forces families to talk. A client will need to talk with the older members of the family to get the past and talk with the younger adults to get the present information. The older generation may not have an accurate picture of the younger family members because of the rule of family secrecy. They often say, "Don't tell Grandmother. She won't be able to handle it."

The structure of family trees and genograms can take many forms. Use what works the best for you. Figure 8.3 is one I use with clients to begin with.

FAMILY ADDICTIONS TREE

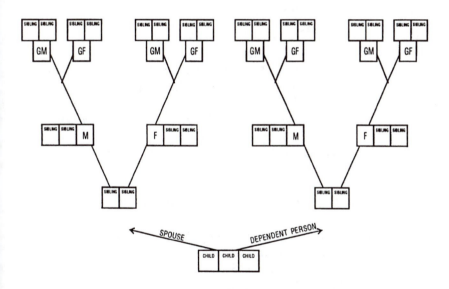

USE THE APPROPRIATE SYMBOL FOR EACH FAMILY MEMBER:

○ ENABLER   ◇ EMOTIONAL PROBLEMS

□ DEPENDENT   △ RIGIDLY RELIGIOUS

Figure 8.3. Family addictions tree diagram.

Directions for Genograms

The directions given here for Figure 8.3 will give you a clear picture. However, you may find it necessary to add other addictive behaviors to the picture such as eating disorders, gambling, workaholism, and sex (when looking at sexual addiction, consider heterosexuality and homosexuality as well).

1   *Connect the "Spouse" and "Dependent Person" arrows to their proper places of birth order (left to right, oldest to youngest), and write in "B" or "G" for both.*
2   *Use the other sibling boxes to put a "B" for boy and "G" for girl in each. Put the "B's" and "G's" by birth order, moving left to right, oldest to youngest. (Add more sibling boxes or leave sibling boxes empty as needed.)*
   a   *Where there is a sibling death, put the "B" or "G" and mark a line through it.*
   b   *Put a "D" over anyone who was divorced.*
   c   *Put an "A" over adopted siblings or write it in.*
   d   *Put a ½ symbol over step-siblings.*
3   *Begin with alcohol and drug problems and mark each with the appropriate symbol (square for dependent, broken square for user).*
   a   *Use a triangle to mark rigidly religious family members.*
   b   *Use a diamond to mark emotional problems.*
   c   *Make up symbols for any other compulsive characteristics (e.g., eating disorders).*
4   *Mark primary enablers (circle).*
5   *Look for patterns. Fifty percent of families will show patterns by this point.*
6   *Go through other dependencies and compulsive behaviors, noting their occurrence in families.*
7   *Look once again for any patterns:*
   a   *Who are the dependents?*
      1)   *Oldest? Youngest? Middle?*
      2)   *Male? Female?*
   b   *Who are the codependents?*
      1)   *Oldest? Youngest? Middle?*
      2)   *Male? Female?*
   c   *Were generations skipped?*

Observations about Simple Genogram

Let us look at an actual family tree (Figure 8.4) and make some clinical observations.

1. *There are a high number of rigidly religious family members on both sides.*
2. *There are a number of dependent middle children both girls and boys.*
3. *In the spouse's family, the dependent middle children were also the youngest of that gender. The spouse's dependent uncle was the youngest of the three older boys, and the spouse's dependent sister was the youngest of the three older girls.*
4. *The dependent's father's side of the family shows the males*

FAMILY ADDICTIONS TREE
CASE HISTORY

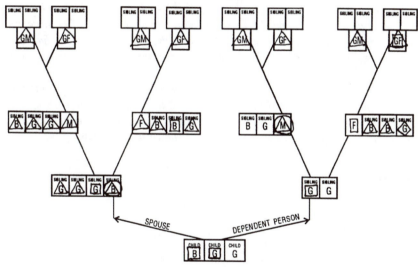

USE THE APPROPRIATE SYMBOL FOR EACH FAMILY MEMBER:

○ ENABLER   ◇ EMOTIONAL PROBLEMS

□ DEPENDENT   △ RIGIDLY RELIGIOUS

Figure 8.4.   Family addictions tree genogram case history.

being prone to addiction. In fact, the firstborn males are prone to addiction, with the grandfather, father, and son all being firstborn dependent males.

Hopefully, you can see the different patterns that exist in this family. Now, the next observation is one to show the true desire for balance. The father's sides have addicted boys in them. Of their children, it is no wonder that the oldest and only son is dependent and the daughter is abusing alcohol. You actually can use genograms as a predictor to speculate which child will be dependent and to look for ways certain children will be treated differently.

In this observation, you can see how codependents and dependents reestablish the family system through marriage. If you are still somewhat skeptical, I suggest you begin to use genograms in your therapy to get some practical experience. You will soon be convinced.

The power behind the use of genograms is that of awareness. First, genograms reveal how the family is addicted—who is dependent and who is codependent. Second, genograms break through denial of both dependency and codependency, while taking the guilt off the individual to a degree and allowing the individual to see the family in a realistic way.

Another simple strategy to use in order to see and understand the balance in families and how couples work to reestablish the system, is to have a client list adjectives describing his/her family members. This can be assigned as homework, as is shown in the following:

Homework Exercise

Father	Mother	Sister
hard worker	intelligent	smart
playful	feeling	hard worker
strong	caring	likes to read
assertive	well-read	assertive
	assertive	

Self	Spouse
playful	intelligent
hard worker	assertive
athletic	hard worker
sensitive	loves to read

You can see that the sister and wife (spouse) have the same character-istics. The mother and wife also have very similar characteristics. So this male client with only one sister found his balance in life with her. When he married, he found a very similar spouse who gave him a sense of balance.

It is most helpful to do this exercise with both individuals in the cou-ple. Quite often the problems can be understood with the list. The hus-band states he is tired of his wife being a know-it-all. When asked what attracted him to her, he says, "She was so intelligent." The list verifies this. So the humorous thing is that he began to resent the very quality he married her for and the quality he denies in himself. He also had similar resentments toward his sister as a child. Clients can easily understand and acknowledge this through the list-making. The new awareness will help the couple adjust the relationship by expressing their positive intents clearly to themselves and to each other.

In recovery, the dependent begins to balance himself/herself by learn-ing to accept and develop all that he/she is. As this occurs, primary siblings and spouses will be thrown out of balance (and will stay out of balance) if they are not in treatment or therapy at the same time.

Hopefully, you can see the need for extended family therapy whenever possible. Without it, the dependent comes under extreme pressure from the different family members to reestablish balance with them in a de-pendent family system. If the dependent remains in a healthy recovery program, removing themselves from chemical use, another family member will often step into the role of chemical abuser. It is important to note that the chemical may change, though the essential pattern does not.

The spouse and children (especially if the children are young) may choose not to become chemical abusers at this time in their lives. In this case, a common result is divorce, with the spouse seeking another dependent mate for balance.

AUDIENCE MEMBER: *I feel I'm an authentic codependent. All my attention is on that.*

(Laughter.)

JIM HOLDER: *I can see your point. Knowing that so many of us are codependent, and have strong feelings of responsibility, I'm re-*

minded of a story. When I was at Esalen Institute in the early 70s, the word responsibility was taken to its max. Being cast in the role of a southern gentleman was interesting while I was spending my time there. I remember one evening, an older female—possibly in her early seventies—came in; she had large suitcases, a number of them. As I stood looking at some books on a bookshelf, I overhead her say to some of the employees checking her in that she needed someone to help her to get to her room, take her things, and show her the way. At Esalen, they didn't pamper people. They considered themselves a hotel; you were basically responsible for yourself. You were responsible for the things that you brought. They shared with this older lady that these were her things and she would be responsible for taking care of them and for finding her own room. Of course they told her where it was, but she would have to follow directions. They snickered a little and looked over out of the corner of their eye at me, for they knew I was still struggling with the concept of personal responsibility—where mine stopped and others' began. Of course I had been there for quite a while. They knew me, so they smiled and said, "Perhaps Jim will be glad to show you." But I grinned back, knowing what they were doing and that they were playing with me. I helped the lady with her baggage and took her to her room. I had a short talk with her and explained personal responsibility to her. It was only a few days later that I was in the office once again, looking at some books, when a blind man walked in. As the blind man checked in, he asked the employees if they would show him to his room. And once again, with the same response they had with the older lady, they let the gentleman know that he would be responsible for himself and that he would need to take care of that himself. They glanced over at me, and with a large grin on his face, one of the young employees said, "Jim might be willing to show you to your room." I grinned again, shaking my head, and said I'd be glad to, and I walked the gentleman to his room. After putting his suitcases in his room, and him feeling rather comfortable, he walked back with me part of the way to the cafeteria. The two of us stopped and sat on the rock steps for a short discussion. I shared with the man that the idea was for people to begin to become more and more responsible for themselves. I would show him down to the cafeteria and help him walk around a little. And from there he would need to begin to take responsibility for himself, in order to find his way back to his room and his way back to the cafeteria. He seemed to understand. After it was over, I shook my head once again and just laughed to myself, thinking that not only the employees but also the Almighty might have been wanting to teach me something about personal responsibil-

ity. So I began to understand. And today, I find it much easer to give responsibility that belongs to my clients—to my clients.

In treatment, it is important to assist clients in understanding how they addicted themselves to substances, people, or behaviors. Equally important is to show them how to recover themselves.

REFERENCE

Wegschieder-Cruse, S. (1989). *Another chance: Hope and health for the alcoholic family.* Palo Alto, CA: Science and Behavior Books.

Chapter 9

UNSOUND RECOVERY
AND RELAPSE

*The essence of personal responsibility is finding ourselves repeat-
edly in the same negative situations until our own personal awareness shows us how to exist in harmony with the world.*

In this chapter, we are going to look at the recovery process from different
personal angles. You might call this our "troubleshooting" section—so instead
of focusing on how troublesome our clients are in their recovery, we are going to hone in on the trouble that is of our own creation. Much of the work
that is being done in *relapse prevention* today is geared toward the recovering person—and that is good—recovering people need to assume personal
responsibility for their ongoing sobriety. However, there may be ways in
which we as professionals actually are contributing to unsound recovery and
relapse.

The addictions treatment field is staffed by professionals from two basic
backgrounds: those who are themselves recovering from chemical dependency
and those who grew up in chemically-dependent or otherwise codependent
families. This is no secret to any of us, for we comprise the vast majority of
the field's professional population. So for the purposes of this section, let us
agree that most of us in the field have our own dependency or codependency
issues.

THE RECOVERING CHEMICALLY-DEPENDENT PROFESSIONAL

It is certainly safe to say that this group of professionals is unique in their contributions to the treatment field. From one-on-one client work to advancements in treatment philosophy, this group can be accorded singular praise and honor for their outstanding work. A majority come from Alcoholics Anonymous and have been extremely useful in this field owing to their depth of personal experience and the remarkable bond that chemically-dependent persons share. And in addition to helping formulate the philosophical foundation for long-standing and successful treatment models, this group maintains an emphasis on personal responsibility and the "hows" of recovery—the best examples of which are found in the 12 Steps.

Unfortunately, this group has worked at great personal risk as well, for their sobriety can be threatened working in a professional environment. It is all too easy for recovering professionals to lose their focus on their own recovery while focusing on assisting others. With ever-increasing pressures from hospital and program administrators, insurance carriers, regulatory agencies, and the like, these people routinely find themselves in high-stress positions. In some situations, recovering professionals lose the integration they had approached in their sobriety, becoming what we referred to in Chapter 3 as "dry drunks"—disintegrated individuals living in their inactive states, fearing their active sides. The prevalence of these at-risk professionals has even given rise to what is now practically a majority statement: that the active side of the chemically-dependent person must be destroyed rather than reintegrated.

No group bears complete responsibility for this; indeed, much of this is owing to the fact that the idea is now being taught to new counselors and further promulgated. It has become a major problem in the treatment business, however, because it is just not the message we want to give clients. The very idea of "destroying a beast" that is in fact part of ourselves should be reprehensible, and instead it is growing in our ranks. We want to talk about forgiveness and self-acceptance, not repression, depression and further denial. If recovering professionals have not forgiven themselves, then they become virtually incapable of sharing the concept with others.

After she worked through her resentment toward her alcoholic mother and found forgiveness, a client referred me to Dr. Martin Luther King's book, *Strength to Love* (1963). In reading it, I was amazed at the relevance Dr. King's words would have for my work.

We must unflinchingly face the fears and honestly ask ourselves why we are afraid. This confrontation will, to some measure, grant us power. We shall never be cured of fear by escapism or repression, for the more we attempt to ignore and repress our fears, the more we multiply our internal conflict. (p. 117)

With this inner conflict multiplying daily, offering our clients an unsound foundation for recovery ultimately will result in physical sickness, the Dry Drunk Syndrome, switching addictions, or relapsing into the original state of active addiction.

THE CODEPENDENT PROFESSIONAL

This group of professionals has intentions of solid gold. What is more, this group has been essential in expanding the scope of treatment for chemically-dependent persons and extending treatment goals into family therapy, workplace relations, sexual abuse issues, post-traumatic stress, codependency itself, and more. By offering a more objective and holistic view of chemical dependency, these professionals have made more complete recovery possible for the addict. And by offering a wider view of who exactly is impacted by the problem, and how whole systems are affected, they have given us a clearer idea of who is sick and how they can get well.

At the same time, many of these professionals continue to labor under the resentment of their own unresolved family issues. For instance, one carryover from codependent family life is the fear of abandonment. These professionals can suffer from an inappropriate need for acceptance by the clients they serve, because they expect and want to guard against any disfavor and chance of abandonment, or they can have their personal resentments triggered by their dependent clients.

Codependent persons become so expectant of the upcoming crisis, that they often live in fear of it. And by changing their focus from the client to the crisis, they actually contribute to making the crisis happen for the client. This creates a cycle of crisis—and of course it is not limited to client relations either. Ask any member of a treatment team to give you a short history of the center where they work—what you will hear is a litany of crisis, one after the other, rather than a movement from one level of success to another.

Of course, this is a generalization. We have all known people coming into this field who, when confronted with triggers from their own unresolved issues, have gotten into therapy themselves or otherwise dealt with their issues, becoming extremely valuable counselors (and happier human beings) in the process.

CHANGING OUR CONFRONTATIONAL STYLES

Recovering dependent and codependent professionals certainly have issues that are crisis-centered. Is it possible that in working with our clients, we subtly conspire with them to create crises through our counseling styles? This way, everyone feels at home.

Look at the way we confront clients, with power and assertion, attempting to "break through" their denial. Haven't their families and friends been trying similar methods unsuccessfully for years? Dependent persons become experts in power struggles, "professional fighters" we might say. Aren't we stepping into the addictive, crisis-ridden world when we confront people this way? Could it be that the reason for this aggressive style of confrontation is a continuation of the crisis-mode of existence that so many of us learned in our own addictions and addictive families?

When we persist with confrontation, a client will often side-step us, saying "OK, I'll go along with what you say." This is usually a passive-aggressive setup, though, for when the client fails, guess who the client claims is responsible—us, the "professionals."

As professionals, we must instead side-step the dependent person's desire for a fight (and sometimes our own, as well) and return the responsibility for recovery to the client. When we aggressively or angrily confront the client, we allow him/her to focus his/her attention on our emotional state, away from his/her own. Argumentative confrontation is *rescuing.*

SEVEN RULES FOR THE BREAKING

In 1981, Sharon Wegscheider-Cruse (1989) put forward seven "Rules in the Alcoholic Family" in her book *Another Chance*. It may be possible that at times we as professionals continue to operate by these same rules in the very treatment centers in which we work. Perhaps it will be helpful to use these ideas as a checklist to make sure that we do not slip into our old patterns of behavior.

Her first rule is *"The dependent's use of alcohol is the most important thing in the family's life."* Is the chemical and its use still the most important aspect of our treatment program? Can we shift our emphasis away from the chemical and focus instead upon the health and integration of the individual? Once the client is abstinent, we must focus on positive goals.

Rule number two is *"Alcohol is not the cause of the family's problem."* This is denial, plain and simple. Usually, many of us in the field have a pretty solid grasp of this concept, so it is not as much of a persistent problem. We must remain on our guard; it can be amazing how quickly we can return to a fantasy to protect ourselves from the truth, particularly if a counselor on staff falls into chemical use. Then, the confrontation must be swift and powerful.

Wegscheider-Cruse's third rule is *"Someone or something else causes the alcoholic's dependency. He [she] is not responsible."* Counselors often show signs of living out this rule in several ways. All of us have heard coworkers blame a family member for a client's chemical use. It may be said in family group, or it may be said as a private joke after-hours. Ever heard this one before? "If I were married to him/her, I'd be drinking myself." Another way we blame others is to act as if the internal voice of the client is something other than the client. When we call the client's active side a "Demon," or a "Monster," or we encourage them to call it "My Addict," we separate the client from a vital aspect of himself/herself and deny his/her integration. Finally, we act as if that separate part of the client is responsible, as if the client himself/herself were not actually using the chemical or acting under its influence. In this way we encourage the client to avoid assuming personal responsibility for his/her recovery.

The fourth rule, *"The status quo must be maintained at all costs,"* is a rule we adhere to when we confront the dependent person on his/her own terms. Again, by subtly conspiring with the client, we perpetuate a crisis-based system that we ourselves need to get out of.

Rule number five is *"Everyone must be an enabler."* This is one rule that we constantly are dealing with as professionals. I regularly hear counselors point out to each other ways in which they may be enabling their patients. The means by which we can enable our clients are too numerous to list; however, I can offer a few rather extreme examples.

In some cases, a counselor begins using enormous amounts of energy working with one particular client. This can include heavy confrontations with shouting and swearing, and inattentiveness to other clients. The counselor in such a situation begins to feel that they are primarily responsible for the client's recovery.

Another example of professional enabling occurs when a counselor over-looks program rules and covers up for the client. In inpatient settings, we routinely see counselors looking the other way to avoid discharging clients for sexually acting-out. In fact, this can spread among the patient community and through the staff to the point where everyone knows what is going on, but no one is talking about it.

This leads us directly to the sixth rule, *"No one can discuss what's going on in the family, either with one another or with outsiders."* On one hand, this is a rather "advanced" rule and usually occurs when other rules are in place. However, sometimes counselors will assume a voluntary code of silence, keeping information out of staffing sessions or treatment team meetings, rationalizing this in the name of keeping the client's confidence.

Rule number seven is *"No one may say what he or she is really feeling."* There are still many counselors in the field who will cut clients off when feelings surface in a session. One of the common ways they do this is through the use of tissues. When a crying client is offered a box of tissues without first asking for them, the "assisting" individual is saying nonverbally, "Stop crying." And the tears usually stop. There are very few clients who will cry or show emotions if the counselor is uncomfortable with feelings. Similarly, when a counselor has personal issues that conflict with something going on with a client (whether religious, sexual, racial, or whatever), clients can be told at every level that it is not okay to talk about these things. Generally, when a counselor maintains a strong feeling about any issue, it can put a damper on a client's expressing feelings.

Please look at all of these rules with an eye toward your own professional practice. First, of course, you will probably notice ways in which your facility has shortcomings; however, awareness is the key to professional growth. One creative idea might be to spend some staffing time coming up with ways designed to break any of these rules that exist.

RELAPSE AS A THERAPEUTIC TOOL

Relapse is not a sign of failure. It only means that the counselor and the client have missed one or more of the client's positive intents.

Imagine for a moment that all of us here are like children in a giant schoolroom, learning lessons and maybe having some fun. The teacher doesn't believe in failure. Repetition, yes; failure, no. In the same sense, the Almighty will give us the same problem over and over again until we learn the lesson it holds for us. Perhaps if we have not learned the lesson in our lifetimes, then we go straight to the teacher and have it explained to us. So relapse is not failure; it is just an indicator that there is more to be learned here.

With all the recent work that has focused on relapse prevention, we may want to shift our focus on the subject. Rather than focus on a negatively-oriented goal of not doing something, let us talk about what we want to *do* *instead*: good relapse prevention is a by-product of quality treatment. P.A.T. is quality treatment that focuses on the positive.

Let us redefine relapse, too. To relapse, a person must first be in sound recovery; that is, he/she must have identified the positive intents underlying both sides of his/her internal conflict, and he/she must be addressing his/her positive intents, moving through the addictive impasse to live a full and flexible life. With this reintegration as the basis of sound recovery, perhaps the number of people who actually "relapse" is much smaller than we would believe.

When a person comes into treatment, we must avoid focusing on the chemical, for the individual can easily switch to other dependencies. The focus should instead be on a full life.

Recently, I was consulted on a case where the client first went into treatment for alcoholism. The client stopped using alcohol, then went to work in the treatment field and quickly became a workaholic. He soon burned out in the work environment, and switched to a sexual addiction in a homosexual relationship. Each time, the crisis took a similar form, with the family in turmoil coming to the rescue. The individual remained unaware of his positive intents for addictive behavior, yet clung to the idea that he was in recovery.

If this person began drinking, would a "relapse" have occurred? P.A.T. says no, because the client never stopped using in the first place. In one form or another, a crisis was ever-present. The individual never reintegrated himself from the internal conflict, and so it raged on, manifesting itself differently over time. Switching addictions is remaining in the addictive pattern, only disguising the appearance.

Using more conventional definitions, when a client switches addictions, it is as if they "relapsed," only the switch is usually difficult to pinpoint in its early stages.

Again, the client and the counselor simply have missed the identification and addressing of one or more positive intents. Simply go back and look at the client's early memories and the guiding fictions he/she shows you. They may be different than those originally discovered, but the treatment process must remain the same: detoxify the client, evaluate early memories to clarify the guiding fictions for living and investigate positive intents, then move to reintegration and a plan for healthy living.

Different faces of the same disease, continued chemical use, switching addictions, relapse, and Dry Drunk Syndromes are all paths the disease may take to shorten one's life. The only way into full recovery is through reintegration of oneself by the accomplishment of positive intents, chemically free. Other than using chemicals, the differences between these forms of addiction is only the amount of time it takes for one to die. There is no way to tell if an active drinker will die from liver failure or an inactive cocaine user will die from a heart attack first. That knowledge is out of our hands; yet we know both cause death to come much sooner than natural. So let us not focus on relapse prevention, switching addictions prevention, and dry drunk prevention; instead, let us focus on integration as a positive recovery process.

REFERENCES

King, M.L. (1963). *Strength to love.* San Francisco, CA: Collins Publications.

Wegscheider-Cruse, S. (1989). *Another chance: Hope and health for the alcoholic family.* Palo Alto, CA: Science and Behavior Books.

Chapter 10

SPIRITUALITY

If what we have learned and felt and seen means anything at all, it means that all of us, whatever our race, creed or color are the children of a living Creator with whom we may form a relationship upon simple, understandable terms as soon as we are willing and honest enough to try.

Alcoholics Anonymous

Spirituality is essential for healthy living, and a good solid recovery process comes only after a person has developed a truly spiritual state of being. The metaphor that I am going to use to explain spirituality in recovery is that of a relationship. Essential in all forms of religion or socialization, spirituality is the relationship between oneself and something greater. Whether that relationship is one with a Judeo-Christian God, one with a more individually defined Higher Power, one with Mother Nature, one with a group, or one with your family, the relationship is all-important. In fact, this is more than a metaphor; the relationship is really all that there is.

Just as we can only see "light" within a context of "dark," we can only understand ourselves as we exist in relationship to others. And our relationship with our own higher power is the primary relationship that will guide all others.

As counselors and therapists, we need ways to detect the level of spirituality the person has reached in the recovery process. I believe this is one area where a large number of therapists become rather confused. It is really quite simple if you stop and see spirituality as an individual process of becoming part of something greater than the self. This process is one of being whole. If we are speaking of an addicted individual, then the individual must begin to integrate all that he/she is and have acceptance for the parts of himself/herself that in the past were enjoyable and the parts of himself/herself in the past that were not enjoyable and may not have been understood.

If you think of the body as a temple, then the first requirement for recovery is to take care of the temple so that the temple is in a state of holiness or wholeness. (Throughout this chapter, when I speak of holy, I am speaking of whole.) So if there are negative thoughts or unholy thoughts, then of course, the individual needs to cleanse the temple of these thoughts (we might call these thoughts "divisive"); likewise, if there are negative substances in the temple, then the individual needs to cleanse the temple and rid it of anything that is causing it to be unholy. So if a client comes in, obviously needing help with addiction and is under the influence, of course you are going to look at a detox process.

Detoxification, then, is a spiritual process. It is one in which the body can begin to cleanse itself. Without the influence of chemicals, the individual can begin to regain a sense of his/her entire self. The goal is one of becoming whole, to be complete within the self.

Notice for a moment how the circle is used in so many spiritual philosophies and religions—whether it is the halo over Christ's head, the circle of the medicine wheel to Native Americans, the Mandala of Yin and Yang of Eastern philosophy, or the circle with the triangle used by AA—the circle is used throughout the world to symbolize completeness. So, when you have a client who still is drinking or using chemicals, it is obvious in this light that the circle is broken. The individual is out of balance. If you take this a step farther into each abusive behavior (whether the person is abusing alcohol and drugs, food, nicotine, sex, or money), if you see in some way that this individual is abusing himself, both mind and body as one, then you know the person is out of balance. In some way, there is a void in his/her life where he/she is denying a part of himself/herself and is filling this void with some substance or behavior.

As therapists, we need to look at quality not quantity. The quality of recovery is related only indirectly to the quantity of time in recovery. So the number of times a person goes to church is not necessarily related to the quality of that person's spirituality. A person could go to church every day, but if he/she does things that are destructive to the temple (meaning that he/she does things destructive to himself/herself emotionally, physically, mentally, in some way) then you know the person has a void in his/her life. In the same sense, if you know an individual who attends a self-help group without ever missing, yet you see this individual putting a substance in his/her body that is harmful, you know that there is something spiritually missing.

Rigid compliance does not equal recovery. Quite the contrary, it may equal relapse or a heart attack. Remember, a large number of alcohol and drug addicts, almost 50% by our study, are fear-based in their perceptions. Fear is in the early childhood memories they offer us. If you see them continuing to perceive from a fear-based standpoint, you know that even though they may have stopped using their primary substance, they have yet to find a way to overcome their fears. They have yet to discover a faith that they have within themselves a Source for the wisdom and strength to walk through life feeling okay with themselves and with others.

RELATIONSHIPS

Let us go back to our original idea, that spirituality is about relationships. The first relationship that needs to be developed is a relationship with the self, because once you have begun to accept yourself and become one with yourself, then you at the same time are one with your higher power. It is paradoxical in nature, because achieving wholeness and establishing a relationship with a higher power is really one in the same. Sometimes we hear members of twelve-step groups saying that theirs is a "selfish" program. It is only selfish in the sense that healthy relationships with others require that we first focus on achieving wholeness within ourselves through self-awareness. At that moment of wholeness, we become open to faith, and we are empowered. With this we find serenity and the joy of self-acceptance.

True self-acceptance implies not only acceptance of yourself as an individual, but also acceptance of a higher power, your friends, your family, and the world in all its conditions.

I have been describing the individual as the temple. In your mind's eye, I would like for you to think about a larger temple that also needs to be held sacred and holy—the temple comprised of the earth and everything on it. It is our responsibility, no matter our spiritual background, to maintain this large temple. There is a great deal of denial and ignorance around this idea. The root word for ignorance means "to ignore." Basically, that is all I am saying. Ignorance is another form of denial. We must look at what we have been given in life and find ways to keep it holy, to be whole with what we have been given. So we must look at our relationship to our environment—all that exists.

So first we looked at a relationship within ourselves. Now, we are looking at our relationship to our environment. The environment referred to is your family, your society, your town, the land on which you live, the air that you breath, all that exists. There are countless ways we choose to ignore or we show our ignorance each day. For a Native American to throw garbage out into a pristine stream would be the same as throwing garbage into the face of his/her higher power. A Southern Baptist who attends church every Sunday and runs a high-volume bingo parlor all night long on Saturday, practices hypocrisy by saying one thing on one day and doing another on another day. There is no difference between these examples and an individual who sees a self-help group as being his/her higher power and steals from the group treasury. Each of these examples shows an individual being disrespectful to his/her higher power, *in the context of the relationship.*

We must begin to take responsibility and become aware of our relationship to all that exists, just the same as we work with our clients to become aware of their relationship with themselves. Awareness is the key. Awareness will take us directly to responsibility for who we are and then acceptance of who we are, in relationship to ourselves, others, and our higher power. Of course, we must begin by becoming aware of ourselves and developing the relationship with ourselves before we do that with the rest of our environment. It is very similar. Just think for a moment in self-help, do you start with the first step and work each through one at a time, doing this over a fairly long period of time? Or do you go from the first step to the twelfth step and begin to help others, avoiding looking at yourself in the process?

I remember an individual years ago who loved to "two-step." He would be in a detox center one day withdrawing, and two days later he would be out doing twelve-step calls. This was an individual that knew how to "talk the talk," but did not know how to truly "walk the walk." Because pretty soon, without integrating himself, this individual would be back in detox as a patient.

Action is itself paradoxical. On the one hand, it needs to be a reflection of an individual's spiritual condition; on the other, it is precisely the thing that enhances one's spiritual condition. While the early members of A.A. discovered that doing twelfth-step work added to their own sobriety, there was also a period of discovery of the need for the first eleven.

So I hope you can see now what I mean when I speak of relationships. By relationship, I mean the relationship between a person's basic parts, understanding and accepting each so that they can become integrated and balanced, so that the person can truly enjoy his/her life. That is spirituality, perhaps in its simplest form—discovering how we fit into the scheme of things with a higher power, if that is how we define that relationship. Likewise, to share a healthy relationship with one's family—this is the reason family therapy is so vitally important. Developing relationships within the family where there is acceptance of other individuals in the family, perhaps even family members who are in addiction, is vitally important. The acceptance and forgiveness that takes place is a step in recovery and is a spiritual step.

Taking this relationship a step further, we can talk about intimacy. Intimacy must begin with a relationship to a higher power, to oneself, to one's family, to one's environment. Since a relationship with the Creator is an intimate one, and with that intimacy comes expectations, many individuals have found themselves to be extremely angry or resentful of the Creator. These are often individuals who have grown up in an organized religion (keep in mind this has been my experience since this is the population with whom I have worked a great deal). These individuals at one time may have lost someone close to them, a child or a parent, and they prayed so hard for God to save this individual, to spare him/her. Some even asked God to take their own life instead of the other individual's because perhaps they were drinking or had done something wrong in their life. Many believe that losing the life of a loved one was, in some way, a punishment for them for the way they have lived.

These are different scenarios that each and every counselor will run into sooner or later if they work in the field very long. We must reminds ourselves that these individuals are people who have grown up in families who believe in others being responsible for them. For some, the "others" becoming responsible for them may have been alcohol and drugs. The alcohol was responsible for giving them courage to speak up in a crowd. Or they could have been from a rigidly religious family. By "rigidly religious" I mean those who made God responsible for their lives. They would pray to God to give them something materially or to make someone better instead of praying to God for the wisdom to work things out. In other words, they wanted God, instead of themselves, to take the responsibility. So if you were brought up thinking that God is responsible for your life instead of *your* being responsible, then of course there will be times when you will be extremely disappointed or you will be extremely confused. This can be an indication of an individual assuming responsibility for something he/she was not responsible for, such as death of a child, thinking it was the punishment of a vengeful God, or that God had somehow mismanaged things.

RESENTMENT/DEMANDS/APPRECIATION

One of the things that we can do to help individuals work through this anger is to have them project onto God and express their anger or resentment for God and actually go into dialogue. This can be a very moving experience for many people. It can be a very moving experience for many counselors. There may be times when you will feel the presence of a higher power in the room when you work. The level of intimacy, while a person is working, can be extreme.

Remember, as therapists, we need to allow clients to work through this, to project onto their higher power, so that they can begin to understand themselves and their own projections, just as if they were projecting onto their father imagining what it would be like to tell their father about something he had done years ago that really upset them. One of the exercises I find to be extremely helpful with this is the resentment, demand, and appreciation exercise. Just make sure that the client expresses resentments held toward his/her higher power, and make sure that the client truly feels the depth of his/her resentment when expressing it. When I have had the hardest time in this process with clients is when I allowed them to go through the process and not actually express their resentments or demands fully. Once they truly felt their demands and resentments, they found it easier to express the appreciation.

An example I recall is a woman who lost her daughter. She resented God for taking her daughter, and she expressed this *resentment*. Basically, she said, "I resent you for taking the life of my daughter when I prayed for you to save her life." She then *demanded*, in a very demanding tone of voice, that God never take another one of her loved ones when she prayed for them to be saved. She then *appreciated* God for not allowing her daughter to suffer any longer than she did. At that moment, there was some relief and acceptance, and the mother was able to go on. That was the first time the mother had ever stopped to look at the flip side of the coin and to realize that she had only looked at the resentment side of the issue and that was where she had gotten herself stuck. She just kept running the resentment tapes over and over again, and she never gave herself a chance to work through the issue.

SUMMARY

It is important for counselors to remember that one does not have to see his/her god or the higher power in the same way clients do. It does not matter.

That is not an issue for us to worry about. We can help individuals work through the issues with their own god or their own higher power by helping them move through this process. This process keeps us out of the loop so that the wisdom will come from within the individual instead of from us and so clients will not become dependent on us. So you help them become dependent upon themselves in order to show them a process that they can use in life to understand how they got themselves in trouble. Once they understand how they got themselves in trouble, they know how to get themselves out of trouble.

As always, we come back to the relationship. We can use two basic guidelines for determining whether an individual is developing healthy relationships—awareness and balance. Remember to apply these two guidelines to the client's two "temples"—there must be awareness within the individual of his/her two parts and an integration or balance between them; but also, there must be an awareness of the larger environment, the individual's relationships with other people and the world, and balance that reflects the integration of the individual with his/her higher power.

Chapter 11

PRACTICAL APPLICATION

Rosalie Holder

Rosalie Hill Holder, MA, LPC, has many of the same counseling credentials as her husband, Jim. Having earned a master's degree in counseling, Rosie has attained certification as an NCAC Level II addictions counselor and is a Certified Master Counselor in the state of South Carolina. She has worked in inpatient treatment settings for more than 20 years and has served on the faculty of two schools for alcohol and drug studies.

"Just as people addict themselves, they can also learn to recover themselves."

EARLY MEMORIES WORKSHOP EXCERPT

ROSALIE: *Is there anyone here who knows the song "Maresy Doates"?* (Those who knew stood and sang the song with me.) *The thing about that song is that if you do not know the words to it, it sounds like it is just a very frivolous, cute little, melodic thing, that really makes no sense. But if we take it a piece at a time, we discover that it does make sense. Because the words are "Mares eat oats and does eat oats, and little lambs eat ivy. A kid will eat ivy too, wouldn't you?" And if you put it all back together it sounds nonsensical again; however, we now know what it means.*

Looking at early recollections is a lot like that. All the study of early memories is, is a tool to help us understand a particular person's frame of reference. The Adlerian term for that is "private logic." Jim used the word yesterday, "filter,"—same thing—"filter," "private logic," "frame of reference." All of us have a unique frame of reference, a unique private logic, and unique filters. Their uniqueness is what makes each of us unique people. We all came up in environments where we were one of a kind; we were the only one of us anywhere.

We look at siblings and wonder how different some siblings can be, all having been raised in the same family, the same parents; how can they be so different? It is because the family system is different with the addition of each new member. I come into the parent's family system and it changes them from two to three; as another sibling comes into that system, it changes from three to four. And all of us who have children know how different we are with firstborns, and second-borns, and on and on. So families change as more children are added.

How we develop who we are is very much dependent on what we see around us, what we hear around us, and how we experience things around us. Someone asked yesterday about how can we be so smart at three years old as to learn so many things about how to be. The thing is that we are really not very smart at three, but we are very alert and aware. We see everything that goes on around us, and hear everything, but we do not have much of a frame of reference developed to filter all this information through. So sometimes what we learn, we learn incorrectly. We learn inaccurately. We might learn for example that there are 10 inches in a foot, and some time later in our adult life, we begin working for a pool company, and we are sent out to dig a hole for a pool that is ten feet deep. The boss knows that there are 12 inches in a foot, but I think that there are 10 inches in a foot. What is going to happen to me? I am either going to have to relearn, or I am going to be out of a job and in a lot of trouble. So it is really important to understand that, in looking at early recollections, none of those things that were learned in those early years are unlearnable. We are reteachable. Particularly when we are doing treatment with people using early recollections, we are finding paths to follow and frames to put things in, understanding that this is a belief the person has, and it was learned as a child, with a child's mind. We are now adults and can look at things with adult minds and decide if the belief is something to be kept, or something to be discarded or changed.

Sample Early Memory

> **R:**   *We will go ahead and begin taking some early recollections, and we need one person to volunteer to share some memories and someone to be the writer* (volunteers in place). *It is important as we do this for everyone to be in a position where you can see Linda* (the volunteer). *Depending on the situation, you may not jump right into doing an early recollection. It depends on how quickly you have built rapport with somebody and what the situation is. In many cases, asking for early recollections is a fairly nonthreatening thing to do. As you are doing a recollection, it is very important to write down word for word what is said. We also have someone else writing it down publicly so all in the room can see it as well as hear it. It is important to get it down as exactly as you can. We will ask for specific memories about* specific *events. Things that start out, "Well, I can remember we used to always go down to the pond to swim every afternoon." This is too general a situation; this is not what we are talking about. What we should be more interested more in is, "Well, I can remember one day when 5 of us went down to the pond to swim, and. . . ." So it needs to be a specific situation that can be visualized and remembered. This technique can be used in any stage of treatment.*

(Linda gives some vocational and personal information to begin and then this memory.)

> **LINDA:**   *I remembered this in a dream, but I asked my mom about it, and she said it was exactly as it had happened and she was surprised that I remembered it so well.*
>
> *When I was five years old, my mother was in Florida, and my father piled us into the back of a black car to pick up my mother. And while we were there we went to Miami Beach, and I remember standing under a palm tree, on grass, looking out at the widest, white sandy beach I had ever seen in my life. It was the first time I had seen white sand. And I had a plaid bathing suit on, and my mother was putting one of those inflatable horses around me. And I remember looking over to my left and there was my dad, standing there leaning against a tree, smoking a cigarette. And there was my mom down with me helping me play with toys. The wind was blowing.*
>
> **R:**   *One question you will want to ask about this is, "If you were watching this as a movie, and you could stop frame at any one partic-*

ular place that really stands out to you, where would it be in this recollection?"

L: *Where I was standing looking out at the sand.*

R: *And what was the feeling associated with this memory?*

L: *Pleasure and contentment.*

R: *So these are the two questions we ask about this: (1) What is the frame that stands out, and (2) What is the feeling associated? Linda has given us a lot of information, a lot of detail. What we do with this is begin to make some guesses about Linda's private logic, things that are important to her, the way she interacts with things around her, and the way she interacts with people around her. We do this by making suggestions to her, i.e., "Could it be that . . .?" And always leave it up to Linda to let us know if the guesses are accurate, to tell us if we are right or wrong. We must remember that as we are doing this, we are doing it out of our own projections. We have her information, but we are still working from our own private logic. We put ourselves in the situation, and say how it would be for us, and that may not be at all true for how it was for Linda. So we need to be very aware of letting her make the decisions and aware of our being able to back off and trying another avenue. I look at projections like mirrored sunglasses, which none of us like to see in treatment centers. It is like having those glasses on with the lenses reversed, and we look out at others through our own reflections first before we can get to anybody else. And I think that is what training is all about. It is broadening our own percep-tions, so we can see others more clearly and with more options. So one thing we might say about Linda, based on your recollection, is that you may be a very visual person; you pay attention to details. You talk about a "black" car, a "plaid" bathing suit, and there was "white" sand. You saw things; you used the word "see" several times. We all access the world in different ways. Some are more visual, some more auditory, some more emotional, and it seems that you like to see things. You like to understand what things are about visually. I wonder about interior decorating with your home?*

L: *I love interior decorating. I like to set things up so that I can use all my senses. . . .*

R: *So she was asked to state a more accurate interpretation about the importance of detail in her life. Because of the way you prefaced* *this memory, i.e., "checking it out with your Mother," I wonder how you are with trusting your own judgement?*

L: *Usually I trust it. I am usually on target with judgement.*

R: *Do you like having people validate your judgement?*

L *Very Much!*

R: *So it is important to you to have people agree with your ideas?*

L: *Yes.*

R: *Again I am making a guess based on how Linda began this memory. "I remember this in a dream, but I asked my mother about it and she said. . . ." This gave us a hint that perhaps she likes someone to say she is right, to stand with her, as her mother was later in the memory. "And there was my mom down with me helping me play with toys." To make a broad statement, when parents are in a recollection, they can be figures, prototypes, for all men and all women in our lives. This will be a real broad guess and we will need to check it out with Linda. Are women nurturers, caretakers?*

L: *Some of them are.*

R: *Is that what you do?*

L: *Yes.* (Linda is a nurse.)

R: *That seems to be what your mother was doing here; she was putting the safety device around you, being there with you, taking care of you. You look back and see your Father standing in the background, smoking a cigarette. So men in your life are kind of out of the picture?*

L: *They sure are!*

R: *And because of the "cigarette," I would ask about Dad's addiction, if any.*

L: *Yes, he was addicted. My Mother was addicted too. They just had different substances.*

R: *Very common for people coming out of addicted families to get into the helping professions—and you are a nurse. Particularly when you want to manage things because things at home were not very manageable. Linda is pretty much acting in this recollection by herself. There are other people there, but you are still pretty solitary, with others being there secondary to the action. Does that seem to fit?*

L: *Yes, that was how it was. I was talking about the sand, and she was just fixing my toys. There was a lot of turmoil in my life then, and this was a time when there was no tension, and I really enjoy the memory. It makes me tearful to talk about this.*

R: *In what way?*

L: *In that it is a little scary to be sharing this personal memory with strangers.*

R: *I really appreciate your doing this. I know it is a tough thing to do. When you do this, you open doors. Sometimes you do not know what is there. So it is a scary thing to do, but it can also be an "aha" experience. You can begin to make sense of things, begin to see a pattern to things. Is traveling an important thing to you? You can get away from the stress and tension of home?*

L: *Yes, when I have problems or something to figure out, I get in the car and turn the radio on and just drive.*

R: *How about men leaning* (father "leaning against the tree")? *Do men lean and women support in your life?*

L: *I certainly chose my first marriage that way. I chose a person who was outwardly big and strong who was going to let me lean on him as I was going through my own problems with drugs, and it turned out that he needed more support than I did!*

R: *Is there something about that memory that you would like to recreate today?*

L: *Yes, I like that feeling of contentment and security. That is what I want for myself as an adult.*

MALE PARTICIPANT: *Why would you remember that?*

R: *There are lessons that are learned from the situations we remember. Or there is something about that memory that fits into the private logic that we still have with us now. Sometimes they can be real horrendous things; sometimes they can be small, minute things. Sometimes there will be very obvious things; other times, things are more covert. And with Linda, it may be important for her to learn how to create order out of chaos—how to find comfort when things seem out of control around her. Again, we need to check our guesses out with people—always check it out. People will give you what is called a "recognition response." Some people call it a "cognitive snap." What that means is that you will see behavior in people when you have made an accurate guess. Their body and their words will let you know when you hit. With Linda, her response to many guesses was to say "sometimes," or "that is almost right." So I wonder if my guesses are not quite on or if Linda qualifies a lot of her answers—not making much definite?*

L: *I want to give more information so you will know about it, and you will understand.*

R: *So it is important for you to be understood? Because if you are understood, things go smoothly?*

L: *Yes.*

R: *You do that really well. You have given us a lot of information about yourself even when it has been uncomfortable to do so.*

PARTICIPANT: *Is it appropriate to ask questions like what would you add to this recollection, or what would you take away from it?*

R: *At some point, it would be appropriate to ask what would be changed about the memory if that were possible. We will talk more about this kind of change work later in the week. We would also ask for a second memory.* (Linda chose not to give a second memory. She said that someone else might want the pleasure of the experience.)

R: *So you would like for someone else to have this opportunity?*

L: *Yes.*

PARTICIPANT: *Would you do this like one-on-one or in a group setting?*

R: *Well, I prefer to do it in a group setting.*

PARTICIPANT: *Let's say you had a residential place and you had 50 clients. How would you choose the group? Would you choose a special group, or would you have the whole group come down?*

R: *Fifty people? Probably for the benefit of the person, I would not do it in front of everyone. Particularly if there is no history together. If you do it in a therapy group that has been established, then that would be a fine place to do it.*

PARTICIPANT: *But how would you set it up?*

R: *Okay, I would do it in a mixed group, if that is available. It would be a fairly randomly chosen group. If people are new in the program, they certainly need to know that this is what we do here, this is how we start, this is your first day, let's get on with it. People who are later in the program, I would hope would have some sensitivity, some guesses; they could help. They certainly could be part of the process. I would want them to know before we started what we were going to do, and make sure the person was not bombarded with things, particularly things that are inaccurate. I would say that anything you have to say to the person certainly turn around and say it to yourself, and see if it fits. Let people know it is important to be supportive and aware of their projections.*

PARTICIPANT: *Working with early memories seems to be getting to the "inner child" and opens the way to do "inner child" work.*

R: *And the additional part of that is that it is still going on with the adult, that it is still going on right here. We are now all that we have been. We are today a culmination of all that we have been.*

L: *Because my training and education requires me to look at details, did I color the memory with details that I remember because of my training as an adult, or was I at five years old that much into details?*

R: *A guess is that the details came first, and you found yourself a profession that helped you live that. And again it can go back to the fact that there were other people and uproar in your young life, and it* *is important for you to put some sense to that, to bring some sense into your own life, to put some comfort into your own life, and control into your life. And to do that, you want to know all the details, all the facts, of your situation.*

R: *Linda wants someone else to have this pleasure, but if she had continued and given a second recollection—you will often want to do more than one—sometimes one is like a drop in the bucket. What you get with the second and third is like adding a bead to a necklace—you remember the add-a-bead necklaces?—it's like adding a bead to the string, and it is the string that we are looking for that runs throughout the life. With more recollections we are looking for validation of things we have already guessed, or we will see any differences. Then we can question the difference and find out what happened to make the difference.*

PARTICIPANT: *Would it make any difference whether they told you positive or negative memories? You know how an addict will tell you that he only remembers bad things; there were no good things?*

R: *Hopefully that kind of attitude would show up in the memory. In Jim's experience he has seen addicts primarily report negative memories and that is part of the development of the addictive lifestyle.*

Let's talk about real memories. Recently I have been reading about the False Memory Syndrome, where people are getting into treatment, and all of a sudden, they are remembering sexual abuse. People are questioning, "did it really happen?" Did the therapist plant the idea somehow? In doing this kind of work (that is, collecting memories), particularly when somebody is fresh into this, when they sit back and decide what they will reveal and what they will not, it does not matter whether this occurrence actually happened or not. It does not matter if this thing really happened to you or not. Things that we remember could very easily have been ways we put ourselves into a story we were told, it could have been a fantasy that we somehow made real for ourselves, it could have been a dream that we made real, or it could have been something that happened to someone else and we put ourselves into it. It can be all kinds of things. I think it would be really interesting to do early recollections with families, with siblings. Particularly if they remember the same things. It could be the same event, and the memories would be totally different. Each person would have learned something different from the same event.

PARTICIPANT: *What if you get someone who can only remember fragments?*

R: *That would be important information in and of itself. It does not have to be a complete memory. Linda gave us a lot of detail in her memory. She wanted us to understand, and she wanted to give us structure. These are important things in her life, so that is how she gave us her recollection. And she gave it quickly, really fast—let's get on with it! That reflects Linda's style. People who give fragments may not attend much to detail or they don't want to reveal too much of themselves. Or it could be that there were things during those years that they decided that they just were not going to remember. We are looking at this on two levels. One is the obvious, what is up here in front of us; that is, the details of the memory itself or the content of it. The other is the style of the recollection presentation.*

PARTICIPANT: *Does it matter if it is the earliest memories or just a significant memory?*

R: *The "Masters" of this art would indicate that there is more to be gained from less traumatic things that are remembered. If people remember, "when I was five years old and the apartment complex I was living in caught fire and burned down." There is information to be gathered in that memory; however, that is an incident that would be really hard not to remember. That would certainly make an impression as you are standing there watching this tremendous blaze—who wouldn't remember something like that. But perhaps if you remember something about what you did as that was happening, there would be more information garnered from that. But you need to take whatever is there, and chances are that will lead you someplace else.*

R: *Another way to begin getting "meat" from the recollections is to ask for a headline that would describe the recollection in a few words. We are checking out what stands out, what is important. Another way to further understand the recollection is to ask people to finish these sentence fragments in relation to the recollection: I am _____, Others are _____, Life is _____. This has to do with what the Adlerians call the "Life Tasks" that we need to learn to handle. It has to do with who am I in this world, who am I in relation to people of the opposite sex, who am I in relation to other people socially, and how do I live in this world and what do I expect from others. How do I live in this world? How do I contribute to this world? Do I give or* *do I take? So we are looking at who I am as a sexual being, who I am in relationship to other people, and who I am in performing good works in this life. We all know people in treatment, and in "real" life, who see the world through rose-tinted glasses—they look outside and all they see is good stuff. I had a fellow in my group not long ago who just saw the opposite. And in the following analogy, I said the nasty word, I said, "you see the world through shit-covered glasses." He agreed, and when he looked outside, instead of seeing the sun and the trees and the birds and all that, he saw all the air pollution and everything else negative.*

PARTICIPANT: *Does that change with whatever phase of treatment you are in?*

R: *I hope so!*

PARTICIPANT: *Is it important to write down the recollection?*

R: *Yes. It is important to write down as much of it verbatim as you can.*

PARTICIPANT: *Do you write it down for your records?*

R: *You should write it down for your own use. You will not accurately remember the details if it is not written down. You will begin to develop your own shorthand as you do it more and more. And it is important to have another person writing the memory for the group to see on a board—both of you together will get most of the memory.*

WORKSHOP RECAP

This section is a consult that took place between Rosalie and Jim after the workshop. The subject was Linda's first memory.

J: *It's always good to take time to go over early memories after a session is over to look in more detail. It's also a great idea to have a consult and to have another individual go over the memories. By doing that, you'll have people looking at it from two different perspectives. The first thing that I noticed is that her father is off to the left, smoking* *a cigarette. That some drug is involved in her first memory. You said that you asked her whether or not she was dependent.*

R: *She said later that she had some trouble with chemicals in her life.*

With perceptual adjustment therapy, we always are looking for the bridge between the early memory and addiction. This is a very positive first memory, and there are positive feelings and very positive outcomes. Yet with this positive memory, the bridge is actually the nicotine that her father is smoking—there is actually a drug being consumed in the memory. You will see that happen quite often also.

CONCLUSION

Let me offer you a few questions to ask yourselves about your clients' early memories—just things I have learned to look for, ideas, typical parallels, and so forth:

1. Is there a problem? Is it solved?
2. Does the person in the memory move toward or withdraw from something?
3. Is the person active or passive?
4. What is the issue of responsibility; is the person being responsible for someone or is someone being responsible for them?
5. What is the place of emotions? Are there emotions shown?
6. Is there rebellion or conformity? Is it open or hidden?
7. Are there other people involved, solitary or with company?
8. It seems that when a person talks about his/her father in a memory, we can make some generalizations about men.
9. Are there obstacles identified?
10. Look for hints of profession. People who have recollections of illnesses or sickness may be in the medical profession.

In addition, here are some questions, Jim uses in working with addicted patients in P.A.T.

11. Is a chemical being used in the memory? If yes, by whom? What sex is the person who is using?
12. Is the memory fear-based or negative?

13. Is there an incongruity between action and feeling in the memory (does anything appear negative that to the client feels positive)?
14. Are substances being consumed that would lead to other compulsive behaviors (e.g. Is food being consumed?)?
15. Is the kitchen the primary room in the memory?
16. Are sexual behaviors being exhibited (possible sexual addiction)?
17. Is a bedroom the primary room in the memory?
18. Does the memory involve working? Is there a possibility of workaholism or switching addictions to work?
19. Is an office or work environment the primary room in the memory?
20. If the recollections of an addicted person are positive, ask if something traumatic happened later in life.

Through the years, counselors will have numerous clients who only show for the first session. When the counselor has done early memories during this first session, during the assessment period, and then there is a no-show, the counselor can see that the memory work is a possible reason why the client did not show up again. It may be that there is a male counselor and the client is a female who is afraid of males, or the client is male and is scared of everyone, or the client has the belief that only his/her friends can get him/her out of a rough situation. Whatever the reason, the first memories may give the therapist some indication of a metaphorical significance of the no-show. With this information, the counselor can make a simple phone call that will serve as an intervention for this client, and either can support the client to come back in and see the same counselor, or can refer the client to a male or female counselor who fits the client's belief system more appropriately. So if, for example, a female client feels more comfortable with males and you are a female counselor, it may be most appropriate (if the client agrees) to refer her to a male counselor in the agency in which you work; if you are a private practitioner, refer her to another private practitioner.

Chapter 12

THERAPEUTIC TECHNIQUES

SEVEN SKILLS FOR SUCCESS

The differences in success among many counselors lies in counselors' abilities to use a few specific skills. These skills are the natural legacy of the great therapists who have preceded us in our field. By "natural," I mean that even to those who lead the way for us, these skills have been brought up and delivered from an unconscious level. Paradoxically, these skills also are learned and refined, for as anyone in this field knows, the best therapists are also the most studied and experienced.

This chapter is devoted to your therapeutic skills. By learning these necessary techniques at a conscious level, we may resonate what is already natural for us at an unconscious level. Practice and experience will develop our skills, and the result will be greater success with our clients.

Consider briefly what it was like learning to drive a car. At first you had to focus on each integral task, constantly keeping the goal in mind, sometimes making mistakes, overcorrecting, and so forth. Now, however, most of us are quite capable of driving down a busy highway at 65 miles per hour, hardly thinking about what we are doing. We may be busily engaged in conversation, singing along with the radio, or thinking deeply about the people we're leaving or going to see. Yet we keep the car on the road at a constant speed, switching lanes when necessary, passing some cars, being passed by others, all without even noticing that we are doing it. This is because driving has been developed through practice to a point where it takes place largely on an unconscious level.

It is this same fluid, natural feel that we want to have in our therapy, and we will develop it much the same way. Specifically, the skills we will deal with here are

1. assessing physiological states,
2. establishing rapport,
3. pacing and leading,
4. breaking states,
5. dissociating,
6. anchoring, and
7. collapsing anchors

Assessing Physiological States

Assessing the client's state is a vitally important skill when working with an addicted population. The level of internal conflict in an addicted client can be extreme, so getting a clear idea of at what point we are starting is essential if we are to assist the person in achieving integration.

Situation: Dependent client comes in.
Task: Assess client's state (three possibilities).

a   Inactive state—Client is chemically free and has a desire to stop using and to remain chemically free.
b   Active state—Client has a desire to still use chemicals but at the moment is chemically free.
c   Chemical state—Client is under the influence.

First, acknowledge the client. This means to verbally or nonverbally meet and greet the client exactly where he/she is, thereby making initial contact.

In determining which state the client is in, sensory acuity will be important. Make a mental image of the client's physiology. Pay close attention without judgement.

Some visual points to note include are the following:

1. Are the eyes dilated or not?
2. Is the breathing deep or shallow?
3. Are the eyes wide open or squinting?
4. Is the mouth turned up or down?
5. If the eyes are narrow, are there laugh lines or crow's-feet?

6. What's the coloring and venation of the face and neck?
7. Are the eyes moist or dry?

Notice that at this point we are not drawing conclusions. For example, you might notice that the mouth was turned upward at the corners, not that the client was "happy." They may in fact be nervous and overcompensating. For the sake of the physiological picture, save the assumptions for later, after you have taken your visual snapshot. Then make whatever judgements you would, and ask questions to verify or refute them.

Touch the client with a handshake, a hug, or a pat on the shoulder. Is he/she shaking? Does he/she appear weak and unresponsive, or is he/she stiff and rigid?

Now use your sense of smell. Does the client reek of alcohol? Is the client clean? Is he/she wearing too much cologne or mouthwash to mask something? Or is the client overcompensating with unduly "perfect" hygiene.

And finally, engage the client in discussion. Use your auditory senses to decide whether speech is slurred, reaction time is off, tone is abrasive, or any other clues as to whether the client is under the influence. As a last measure (if necessary), come right out and ask if he/she has been using.

If the client is under the influence, you must allow him/her to go through detoxification and become chemically free (including being free from withdrawal-assistance medications) before you can assess the other two states.

Immediately following detoxification, a client often will tell you exactly which state he/she is in without any prompting. For example, he/she might say, "I'm killing myself with these drugs and I have to stop using." Clearly, the client is in an inactive state—unless he/she has positive intent for lying, like if his/her spouse or supervisor were sitting in the room and he/she were conning them.

The active state may be obvious as well. The client may say, for example, "I know I've overdone this thing and I intend to cut down," or " I know I've got a problem with cocaine, but alcohol isn't a problem so I can still drink moderately." In either case, the client plans to continue using chemicals.

Regardless of which state you determine the client is in, it is most important to have a clear mental picture of the state you witnessed for your future work with the client.

Establishing Rapport

Rapport is the foundation upon which all therapy is based. It goes far beyond trust, comfort, or understanding and is perhaps best understood as the conduit through which we can give and receive information with the client.

Situation: Good communication is needed.
Task: Establish rapport.

Step 1   Mirror the client auditorially.
    a   Auditory predicates (terminology, vernacular)
    b   Voice tone and tempo

Step 2   Mirror the client visually.
    a   Gestures
    b   Postures
    c   Breathing

Step 3   Lead the client to confirmation of rapport.
    a   Change auditory and visual aspects.
    b   Observe to determine if client mirrors changes. (When the client follows changes lead by you, rapport is established.)

The basic idea behind this technique, developing rapport, is essential for any kind of quality treatment and therapy.

Understand that these steps have been refined for centuries so that today they are performed by many people at an unconscious level. We present them here broken down into their individual components so that therapists can identify each step and determine if any of their particular adaptations need further work and development.

The first two steps are to mirror the client either verbally or nonverbally. Mirroring means subtly copying the speech patterns, gestures, posture, and breathing of the subject in order to let the person know at an unconscious level that you are "with" him/her.

For example, when two people begin to communicate, one may have his arms and hands arranged in a certain way and begin to speak in a raised tone of voice. The second can arrange his/her hands similarly and raise his/her voice to the same level. As an exercise, you may wish to observe people doing this naturally. Rapport is essentially a dance between two people, so it is important to watch both simultaneously. It establishes an unconscious bond between the participants, making further communication much more effective.

This can occur even if the two cannot see each other. For example, people often mirror each other's physiologies while on the telephone. Basically, if one person mirrors the other's tone and tempo in his/her voice, the breathing will also be copied and then the body will assume a similar physiology. An interesting exercise is to let two people sit back-to-back and have a conversation without looking at each other. While talking, they will begin to take on the same body movements and their communication improves.

To confirm that this bond has been established, a therapist can begin to "lead" a client. The therapist might gesture in a particular way with one hand or shift his/her weight to change posture. In good rapport, the client would then make some change to mirror this within approximately 30 seconds. Remember: Rapport does not mean that someone agrees with you or even likes you; it only means that the person is open to communication with you at this particular moment in time.

Pacing and Leading

Pacing and *leading* a client is the natural first course of therapy. This technique involves shifting another person's state so that he/she may be more or less receptive to certain ideas. Note that this is not changing the person's *mind*; instead, it is more like changing the person's body so that his/her mind can see more possibilities.

We all encounter addicted clients in a state of crisis—think back and remember the rapid speech rate, the shallow breathing, and other characteristics that accompany crisis. In developing rapport, mirroring your client, you adopt a similar physiology and get in sync with him/her. When you begin leading a client, you slow your breathing, and lower the tone and tempo of your voice. This brings the client down with you, so that he/she can see things more clearly and be more open to alternatives.

Situation: Client is in an undesirable state.
Task: Shift client's state by pacing and leading.

Step 1   Establish rapport.
      a   Use mirroring techniques.
      b   Validate rapport by leading client.

Step 2   Determine the quality of the client's state.

Step 3   Fully assume, or pace, the physiological state of the client.
    a   Completely mirror, in every way possible, the client's physiology.
    b   Experience the feelings associated with the client's state.

Step 4   Lead the client from the undesirable state to one that is more productive.
    a   Gradually change multiple aspects of your physiology to more productive ones.
    b   Observe that the client is "following."
    c   Continue this process until the client has achieved a more desirable state.

During the period when you develop rapport and determine the client's state in Steps 1 and 2, you will be pacing the client with your breathing and voice, etc. At the point where you realize you are in rapport, you may then—or at any time you wish thereafter—choose to experience the feelings associated with that state. I caution you to be aware of how long you remain in a less than optimal state. It may not be productive for you to be depressed or angry for long. Once Step 3 is accomplished, you would move to Step 4 and lead the client to a more resourceful state by changing your physiology. Alter your breathing, your body, and your actions; then observe the client to see that he/she follows.

Everyone already has some skill in pacing and leading. Now, with a conscious understanding of it, you can be more productive in your therapy; also, you can avoid being paced and lead by your client into a less than resourceful state where the two of you can be stuck for the entire session.

It is important to realize that an unproductive state in one situation may be a productive state in another. An aggressive, angry state may be very productive if someone were threatening violence. Also, a state may not need to be maintained for a long time. Simply changing someone's state to allow him/her to achieve something (crying, for example) can be remarkably brief and at the same time cathartic and powerful.

Breaking States

P.A.T. deals with physiological states to such a degree that we must learn to reorganize states, hold states that are needed, and break states when necessary to enhance the client's capabilities. ***Breaking*** a client's ***state*** is a time for your own spontaneity and personal creativity to truly come into play. There are times when clients are in such a nonresourceful state that you need to take immediate action.

Situation: Client is in an undesirable state.
Task: Break client's state.

Step 1   Establish rapport.
     a   Use mirroring techniques.
     b   Validate rapport by leading client.

Step 2   Determine the quality of the client's state.

Step 3   Directly intervene in the client's state.
     a   Verbal—use loud, quiet, funny, aggressive, caring, and/or unconventional language.
     b   Nonverbal—make a funny face, strange gesture, or unusual action.

Step 4   Observe the client's physiological state change.

Think of a depressed person and how he/she sits in a chair in your office. Pay close attention to how he/she breathes shallowly, the posture with the head and shoulders down, etc. We all have seen clients like this, and I can tell you that asking them questions regarding their positive intents about anything is futile while they are in this state.

For example, ask, "What is the best thing that has happened to you lately?" and clients might say "Nothing." They are not misleading you on purpose. From that state of depression, they may lack completely a way of recalling positive events. Or, if they do remember one, they would not experience any positive emotions associated with the recall because the feelings themselves are depressed.

A state break can be anything from a physical movement designed to change the client's physiology. to a sudden out-of-character behavior—an angry tone of voice, for example. Anything that changes the client's physiology will change both his/her feelings and his/her attitudes. Several general types of state breaks include humor, gestures, touching, odd tones of voice, singing, whispering, moving, and countless others.

To go back to our example of depressed clients, you would want to raise their head and shoulders and improve their breathing. Simply getting up from your desk can force them to raise their chins to follow you with their eyes. As they do this, they will naturally breathe more deeply, receiving more oxygen. This will contribute to a state that is more balanced, more awake, and more receptive to more emotions and will allow them to have visual recall of more positive events.

Dissociating

Clients often are *dissociating* from their feelings. Rarely can you watch a group work for more than a few minutes without seeing a group member dissociate from something important. The dissociation may be as simple as pulling one's head back, leaning back in a chair, sliding one's chair back, or getting up and walking out of the circle. Each of these actions is usually a form of dissociation from one's emotion. Basically, the person is saying, "You've gotten too close to something I have strong feelings about, and I'm uncomfortable."

Situation: Client is in an undesirable feeling state.
Task: Change client's state using dissociation.

Step 1   Establish rapport.
         a   Use mirroring techniques.
         b   Validate rapport by leading client.

Step 2   Determine the quality of the client's state.

Step 3   Dissociate the client from the undesirable state.
         a   Ask the client to imagine himself/herself in another place—across the room, for example.
         b   Ask the client to feel himself/herself as if he/she really were physically in exactly that place.
         c   Ask the client to imagine tapping his/her feet or thigh—and hearing it.
         d   Ask the client to leave all his/her complaints in a box right there and to come back here.

Step 4   Notice the change in the client's physiology.

To understand how this works, you must first understand that when most people are *in* their feelings, they are leaning slightly forward, looking down toward the right, body tilted to the right, breathing deeply. They also may have the right foot or leg out in front or over the left, using the right hand or having it on top of the left. The right side of the body tends to be more feeling oriented, the left side more auditory—at least for the majority of right-handed people. (Yes, lefties may be the opposite.) Visual orientation tends to have an upward tilt either from the eyes or head. Therefore, when you see individuals get *out* of their feelings, you will see them move in one of these other directions. They may, for example, lift the head up, lean back, pull the right leg under the chair, or cross it with the left and breathe more shallowly. At this time, they may have moved into an internal dialogue or begun to visualize instead of feeling.

We all know this on some level. When a person is upset, we say "Keep your chin up." We mean, of course "Dissociate yourself from those feelings."

As an exercise, observe how people stop crying. They first will dry their tears; then they turn their eyes, and usually their heads as well, upwards. When a group member offers a crying person a tissue, the member is giving the crying person a suggestion—to dissociate from those feelings (usually because the member offering the tissues is pretty uncomfortable, too).

Like everything else, there are times when it is important and even healthy to dissociate from feelings. For example, a client may be stuck in negative feelings or overwhelmed by them and need a more productive state from which to work.

Once a client can see himself/herself in another place, feel himself/herself there, and hear himself/herself there, the client is no longer aware of the feelings he/she had in his/her body. And at that moment, the dissociation is complete.

Finally, as a way of checking your work, you can look to see if the physiology has changed while you ask the client what he/she is experiencing. You also can teach your client this technique to use on his/her own whenever appropriate.

I once had a female client who, every night when her husband came home, would have to have an argument at the door. By using this technique (imagining herself across the room), she was able to get out of her feelings at the moment he came in. He noticed the change in her physiology and, looking confused, briefly left the room. He returned a minute later and had a nice discussion with her (which they both desperately wanted anyway). So by learning this technique in one brief session, this client was able to dissociate herself from her feelings at an appropriate time, thereby controlling what had been an uncontrollable emotional situation for her and her husband.

Dissociation is a valuable tool with many practical applications, especially in the area of breaking behavior patterns that are emotionally centered.

Anchoring

Since the beginning of recorded time, *anchors* have been used to bring thoughts, memories, or feelings into the conscious awareness. A couple may be dating and have a song play during a peak experience, and from that point on, any time they hear this song, they remember that particular moment and the feelings associated with it. Years may pass; in fact, their partners may change, yet when they hear that song, they once again experience that moment with the other. This is because the state has been anchored, and the song is the *trigger* or *anchor*.

Anchors are basically of five types: auditory, visual, olfactory, kinesthetic, and chemical. It may be important to note that chemical anchors are by far the most powerful and are thought by some to be near the heart of addiction.

Setting, firing, and collapsing anchors is a simple process; however, many of us in the field have often overcomplicated this concept and made it seem difficult.

An anchor is any stimulus that brings a person back to a specific thought or its related physiological state. During a workshop, I once chose to demonstrate the idea using a volunteer who was having a particularly difficult time understanding it. I asked her to think of a time when she was in a state of excellence. After she had closed her eyes and I believed she was experiencing that state, I squeezed her little finger to set the anchor. Immediately, her state changed, and a tear ran down her cheek. Puzzled, I asked what she was experiencing. "Warmth and love," she said. Going on, she told us that when she was a little girl, her mother would squeeze her little finger just the same way sometimes when they sat together in church. It was a secret they had together, and it meant "I love you." So in attempting to set a new anchor of excellence, I inadvertently had fired an older, more powerful anchor from childhood. My particular example had been unsuccessful, but every participant in the workshop then understood exactly what anchors were and how powerful they were in bringing about a physiological state.

Situation: Client is in a desirable state.
Task: Obtain future access to a this state using anchors.

Step 1   Establish rapport.
    a   Use mirroring techniques.
    b   Validate rapport by leading client.

Step 2   Determine the quality of the client's state.

Step 3   If a desirable state, anchor it at or near its peak.
    a   Kinesthetically
        1)   Touch must be precise in area and pressure.
        2)   Touch must be reproducible.
    b   Visually
        1)   Movement, color, etc. must be well-defined.
        2)   Image must be reproducible.
    c   Auditorially
        1)   Tone and tempo must be unusual and well-defined.
        2)   Sound must be reproducible.

To set clear, powerful kinesthetic anchors, you must use the same amount of pressure on precisely the same part of the body. This will be most effective if it is used on a part of the body that is not touched often. For example, the shoulders might not be best, since people often touch each other there, and many anchors from the past have been set there already. I often use the gaps between the knuckles on the hand, or the place right behind a subject's elbow, because these places are easy for me to locate exactly the second or third time and they are usually free from past anchors.

Having mentioned that chemical anchors are the strongest, as addictions professionals, we have our work cut out for us. To use a very typical example, consider a young man who has basic fears of socializing with young women. He visits a bar with his friends and has his first few beers, experiencing the lowered inhibitions the chemical produces. At this point, the anchors that may be set are numerous: the visual anchor of the mug of beer with a head on it; the kinesthetic experience of the frosted handle in his hand; the olfactory aroma; and finally, the chemical anchor of the beer itself. The various physical anchors may trigger a desire for the chemical, while the chemical itself would be the anchor for a state of confidence (due to state dependent learning). The memory of how to act in a state of confidence is also reduced when the chemical is withdrawn.

In setting anchors, you may find the steps outlined above to be helpful. After setting the anchor in Step 3, you must break the state and again fire the anchor to determine whether it has been well-established.

Some examples of anchors follow:

Kinesthetic:
These are the most powerful anchors short of chemicals. Feel any part of the client with your hand so that you can repeat it with the same pressure in the same place. A foot may be used as well.

Visual:
These commonly are used in print media, advertising, and television. Businesses, sports teams, and other organizations go to great lengths to achieve "name recognition" through logos, color schemes, and consistent visual images. If you saw a Clydesdale horse, what would you think of? Similarly, on game day, the students and fans at large universities fly the schools' banners on the way to the game. Each time the fans have another exposure to the image, the excitement increases, and by the time they are at the stadium, they are in a profound state, ready to cheer.

Auditory:
These are equal in power to visual anchors. "Jingles" on radio and television were among the first anchors popularly manipulated by broadcast media. They are used easily in conjunction with visual anchors. The "BOOM, BOOM, BOOM" of the bass drum can conjure the image of an Eveready bunny long before it takes the screen. Television's remarkable influence is related to the synergy it achieves by simultaneously employing auditory and visual anchors.

Collapsing Anchors

Collapsing anchors is a way to decrease the power of a negative anchor, thereby assisting a client in remaining in a more productive state. In fact, in many situations, we can assist clients in nullifying negative anchors altogether by collapsing them into a positive experience.

Situation: Client has unwanted thoughts, feelings, and behaviors.
Task: Obtain a desired physiological state by collapsing anchors.

Step 1   Establish rapport.
    a   Use mirroring techniques.
    b   Validate rapport by leading client.

Step 2   Determine the quality of the client's state.

Step 3 If it is a desirable state, anchor it at or near its peak.

Step 4 Break state and check anchor.

Step 5 Access other (usually less resourceful) state and anchor it.

Step 6 Break state and check anchor.

Step 7 Access both anchors.
    a Set resourceful state first, and hold.
    b Set resourceless state next, hold both.
    c Lift resourceless state first, resourceful last.

Step 8 "Future pace" to check work. If more resourceful physiology occurs, integration is complete.

Part of integration work includes collapsing anchors of a negative situation and a positive situation.

When anchoring a state, it is important to anchor the state at the peak of the person's experience. It is easy to understand if you picture a bell curve that starts off on a low end, rising higher and higher until it reaches the peak and begins to taper back down. When observing a client's physiology, you will be able to hit at or near the peak with a little practice.

After you have set a positive anchor, broken the state, and refired the anchor to check if you see the same physiological state recur, you must once again break that state before going on to the resourceless state. Once you have anchored the resourceless state, you go through the identical process of breaking the state, refiring the anchor and checking the state, then breaking that state again. At this point, the client should be in neither of the anchored states, showing none of the physiology associated with either.

In Step 7, the integration takes place by firing both anchors. Start with the new positive resourceful state to give it more power, and within a few seconds after, fire the resourceless state. As integration occurs at this juncture, you should see some of both states appearing. Often, you will see a shift from one to the other; then you may see a blending of the physiologies. After this has occurred, release the resourceless anchor first; then a few seconds later release the resourceful anchor. The integration will continue for some time.

The last step is to *future pace*—that is, have the person imagine a setting that would have been a problem before, and see if he/she experiences a more resourceful fantasy of possibilities. If the person can imagine a more resource-ful experience, your work is done.

FIVE STRATEGIC INTERVENTIONS

The five strategies chosen for this chapter are the ones we have found most useful in P.A.T. There is, of course, an almost infinite variety possible, combining and recombining the therapeutic skills developed in the first part of this chapter.

Metaphors and Concept Change

The first two of these strategies, *metaphors* and *concept change*, are pow-erful strategies for use with early memories. In terms of creative work, the first is a strategy "keyed" upon the counselor; the second is "keyed" upon the client. A metaphor is constructed by the counselor to confront the client's filter or private logic given to the counselor through the client's early memory. In a concept change, the client does much of the creative work by constructing a new memory to be collapsed into the old. Both have the purpose of opening new doors for the client and challenging the client's private logic.

Situation: Client has a denial of possibilities.
Task: Obtain more resourceful possibilities by using metaphors.

Step 1   Establish rapport.
    a   Use mirroring techniques.
    b   Validate rapport by leading client.

Step 2   Determine the quality of the client's state.

Step 3   If it is an undesirable state with a denial of possibilities, construct a metaphor.
    a   Shallow metaphor
       1)   Present day
       2)   Obvious to conscious and unconscious
    b   Deep metaphor
       1)   Distant past, fairy tale
       2)   Obvious only to unconscious
    c   Punch metaphor

Step 4   Future pace to check work. If more resourceful physiology occurs, in-tegration is complete.

Metaphors are a wonderful therapeutic strategy, and their use in P.A.T. is required because the client will be working using a metaphor of existence, the early childhood memory.

In P.A.T., therefore, the client already has done much of the work for us. We use a *shallow metaphor*, we might simply reframe the early memory for the client, and he/she will understand the work, both on a conscious and an unconscious level.

I remember an individual where a simple reframe like this was invaluable. His memory involved a scene where his parents sat down to tell him that another baby was expected in their family. In the memory, the individual was angered, and this was made worse by the fact that the family was poor. He feared that another baby would not only take his parents away from him, it might use up the family's resources as well. As an adult, the individual always had disliked his siblings and maintained a distance from them.

I reframed his memory by suggesting that his mother and father must have loved him a great deal, that they would sit down with him as a child and talk to him about their plans. The impact was immediate and powerful, as a tear appeared in his eye and he nonverbally agreed. This happened to be a significant turning point for him, and today he is very close to his siblings and involves them in his life.

A *deep metaphor* could be used by taking the events and characters in a memory and shifting them to a fairy tale setting. This moves it more to the subconscious. Consider the following:

> *A long time ago, in a time before man walked on the earth and animals could talk, there was a family of lions living on an island with only a moderate amount of food to sustain them. The lion and lioness had a wonderful cub, and were so pleased with this cub that they wanted another. One of the main reasons they wanted another cub was so that it could play with the one they had, for they knew that in growing up, it is important to have someone near the same age for you to play with. Knowing it would be a hardship, the parents decided that it would be worth it for the joy that it ultimately would bring to them and their cub. The lion and lioness sat down with their cub and told him of their plans, for they loved him so much they wanted to share it with him first. Momentarily, the cub worried about losing his place in the family; then he thought about how much his parents loved him, and he began to imagine all the adventures he would have with another cub.*

He lay in the sun like this, thinking of how much his parents loved him and how much fun they would all have together, until he fell fast asleep.

The third type of metaphor is a ***punch metaphor***. This is usually one word or one line that recalls for the person an idea or belief he/she already has. Have you ever been working with an impulsive recovering person irritated and agitated over the recovery process? Simply saying to them "One Day At A Time" can have a marvelous effect. It is an often-used punch metaphor, as are all of the "slogans" in 12-step groups and treatment programs.

Situation: Client has a history of resourceless behavior or thoughts connected to an early memory.

Task: Obtain more resourceful state using concept change.

Step 1   Establish rapport.
    a   Use mirroring techniques.
    b   Validate rapport by leading client.

Step 2   Identify memory or sequence of memories to be changed.

Step 3   Determine the quality of the client's state. If feelings involved are not overpowering and normal state breaks will be effective, proceed with change history (Step 4).

Step 4   Ask client to imagine the memory to be changed, then anchor the state.

Step 5   Break the state; recheck the anchor; break the state.

Step 6   Ask client to imagine a new memory that has greater possibilities.

Step 7   In the new memory, check physiological congruence.
    a   If incongruent, ask "is there any part of this new memory that you or any part of you doesn't like?"
    b   If congruent, ask them to step into it and experience it physiologically.

Step 8   When the client is experiencing the new memory near its peak, anchor it.

Step 9   Break the state; recheck the anchor.

Step 10   Collapse both anchors (firing new memory first and releasing old memory first).

Step 11 Future pace to check work. If more resourceful physiology occurs, integration is complete.

Concept change is an important part of P.A.T. because it gives the client control over how he/she wants to see things differently. Basically, you take the memory or similar memories and change them to more resourceful ones, giving the client more options in his/her metaphor for life. In terms of techniques, this means anchoring the old memories together with new memories, integrating old and new beliefs.

In Step 3, you must identify the memory to be changed, then decide if the feelings associated with it are overpowering the client. In other words, determine whether the emotional anchors are going to interfere with your work. If the feelings are not overpowering, go on to Step 4. When the feelings are overpowering, use the next of our strategic interventions, Multiphasic Dissociation.

You will notice that all of the following steps are essentially the same as the Collapsing Anchors skill with a few modifications. One change is in Step 6 where you ask the client to visualize a memory without stepping into it. This is sometimes tricky work. We do not want the client experiencing the memory because that would bring on the associated feelings and perhaps set an emotional anchor. We simply want the client to visualize the memory as if it were on a TV screen.

Once the client has designed a new memory, ask him/her if any part of the self disagrees with it. This will require close observation on your part. The client will be in an emotional state. You must watch to see that his/her physiology agrees with the new memory. If there is an obvious inconsistency, or if you even sense that something is unacceptable, ask the client to make changes in the design of the new memory. Congruency is vitally important here. When a client says he/she likes the new memory, his/her physiology should agree. There needs to be some positive appearance or tones about the physiology. Then, after any adjustments have been made, ask the client to step into the new memory and experience the feelings.

Allow the client to reach a peak for experiencing the new feelings associated with it, then set an anchor for the new memory. Having done this, break the state.

Now, fire the anchors for the new memory and the old, one after the other, integrating the two. After a few moments of integration, release the old anchor first and then the new anchor.

Now future pace your work. If for some reason this work has been unsuccessful, you may need to start over. If you do, first ask the client if he/she has an idea of why it did not work—always let the client guide your work.

Multiphasic Dissociation

Multiphasic dissociation is necessary when the client is overwhelmed by negative feelings such as anger, fear, resentment, or pain. You would use the multiphasic dissociation (called *3-step dissociation* by Neuro-Linguistic programmers) to allow the client the emotional space to create new memories.

>   Situation: Client has a history of resourceless behavior or thoughts connected to an early traumatic memory.
>   Task: Obtain more resourceful state using multiphasic dissociation.

Step 1   Establish rapport.
     a   Use mirroring techniques.
     b   Validate rapport by leading client.

Step 2   Determine the quality of the client's state. If powerful feelings are involved, proceed with 3-step (multiphasic) dissociation.

Step 3   Identify powerful resource state and anchor it.

Step 4   Break the state; recheck the anchor.

Step 5   Identify the traumatic memory (or memories) and anchor it.

Step 6   Break the state (completely).

Step 7   Begin multiphasic dissociation. Ask the client to imagine himself seated in the back row of a theater.
     a   Have the client experience the feeling of sitting in the chair.
     b   Anchor dissociated state and hold it.

Step 8   Ask the client to visualize *from his seated position* another image of himself walking down the aisle and taking a seat in the center of the theater.
     a   Still experiencing feeling the chair on the back row (anchor still in place).

Step 9 Ask client to watch himself altering the old memory on the screen.

Step 10 Go back and make sure that the client is comfortable with new memory (or memories). Physiology should be congruent.

Step 11 Reintegration of parts.
- a Have back row walk down to center seat, exchange greetings, thanks, and a hug.
- b Imagine the parts becoming one.
- c Walk up to the screen and step into new picture.

Step 12 Set a new anchor on the new memory.

Step 13 Break the state; recheck it.

Step 14 Collapse anchors and change history—fire both anchors (new memory first) and release them (old memory first).

Step 15 Future pace to check work. If more resourceful physiology occurs, integration is complete.

This strategy is quite useful in working with highly emotional situations or memories.

Once contact and rapport have been established, it is wise for us to find a powerful resourceful state to use as a safety net if we need it. You could ask the individual to remember a time when something wonderful happened and he/she had feelings of power and self-confidence. Once you see the client experiencing this state near its peak, anchor it.

Then, of course, break the state and fire your anchor once again to see if it is well-established and as powerful as you want.

The next step is to have the client imagine walking into a theater and sitting on the very back row, in the middle of the row, and feel himself/herself sitting in the seat with arms on the armrests. Anchor the client in that setting and hold it.

Now, while holding this "back row" anchor (I usually place this on the hand or arm), ask the client to imagine self getting up and walking down the aisle a few rows, then sitting in a center row seat. The client should at this point see himself/herself from behind, sitting in the center of the theater. Instruct the client to feel himself/herself in this situation, watching dispassionately, able to see the old memory on the screen and manipulate it any way he/she wishes without any strong feelings coming out. The only feelings he/she should be experiencing are the tactile impressions of being seated in the back row while watching the self watch the screen with the old memory.

Now instruct the client to develop a new memory, experiencing it on the screen from the back row. When the client does this, you do an ecological check—looking for agreement between physiology and the memory. If this is congruent, ask the client (who is perceiving himself/herself from the back row) to imagine himself/herself getting up, walking down the aisle, and meeting the other image of himself/herself.

If appropriate, you may have two images thank each other or exchange a hug. Just be sure to do something to integrate the parts.

Next, have the client walk down the aisle and step into the screen with the new memory. When the client is at the peak of this experience, set a new anchor, giving the client a short time to enjoy the new memory. Break the state, then fire the anchor once again to check it.

If this looks good, you can move on to a final integration: holding the resourceful anchor, firing the less-resourceful one briefly, and releasing the less-resourceful one after just a short time. Then future pace to finish the work.

Appreciative Reframe

I use a strategy called the *appreciative reframe* when an individual is emotionally stuck and reaches an impasse within himself/herself. Some examples might include the addict's internal conflict over chemical use and its ramifications, or perhaps an unresolved issue with a person who is deceased or otherwise unavailable for reconciliation.

Addicted individuals usually move past such a block when they are under the influence and in a chemical state. However, due to state dependent learning, they have little memory of the expressive skills necessary to do so when they are straight and pull back into their nonexpressive roles.

Our job, then, is to assist clients in experiencing this breakthrough and in achieving awareness of it so that they can recall and reproduce its effects later in their daily life.

A basic cause for many impasses is the fact that the individual has never looked at the positive side of the behavior that he/she resents. He/she may be fully aware of the resentment but has not become aware of an appreciation of its positive side. An appreciative reframe is the solution.

Situation: Client is stuck in conflict with self or others.
Task: Obtain more resourceful state using appreciative reframe.

Step 1   Establish rapport.
a   Use mirroring techniques.
b   Validate rapport by leading client.

Step 2   Determine the quality of the client's state.

Step 3   If conflicted, ask client to visualize the person or part conflict is with.

Step 4   Have the client express resentment in specific terms. Repeat until client sounds and appears congruent in message and physiology.

Step 5   Have the client express the demand that this behavior end, again in specific terms. Repeat until client sounds and appears congruent in message and physiology.

Step 6   Have the client express appreciation for the undesired behavior.
a   Use "because" to identify positive intent.
b   If problems occur, start over, expressing feelings more honestly.

Step 7   Future pace to check work. If more resourceful physiology occurs, integration is complete.

Appreciative reframes can be used with clients feeling that they are in conflict with themselves or others. The reason so many people get stuck in conflict is that they never have examined the other side. Until a person can experience what seems to him/her to be the opposite side of a situation, he/she will not move; without movement, there can be no growth or spiritual life. Perhaps Dr. Martin Luther King (1963) described the goal behind this idea best:

> Forgiveness does not mean ignoring what has been done or putting a false label on an evil act. It means, rather, that the evil act no longer remains as a barrier to the relationship. Forgiveness is a catalyst creating the atmosphere necessary for a fresh start and a new beginning. (p. 48)

The appreciative reframe is a way of moving people to forgiveness. Clients most often can tell you (in great detail) what they resent about a person's actions, yet they come up short when asked to appreciate the action or the positive intents underlying it. Fritz Perls wrote the following:

> Appreciation is the flip side of resentment. One cannot exist without the other. The most important part of this strategic intervention is the counselor's ability to calibrate the sincerity in the resentment and the demand, and the assertiveness to accept nothing less than sensitivity from the client.

So here is the question: When do you ask the person to share their resentment? Whether it is the inactive side talking to the active side, or a client talking to a visualized parent, the client must be congruent in his/her resentment. Once that is accomplished, the client must be congruent in his/her expression of the demand to never do that again. Once the demand sounds, looks, and feels like a demand, you may move directly into appreciation and have the client appreciate what he/she just resented, using the word "because" immediately after describing the demand. Once the client can express the appreciation, personal awareness is experienced.

Internal conflict is usually easy to spot, because it comes with a "but." "I love you, but you are too demanding." The "but" takes away the power of the first statement. A more congruent way of saying this might be, "I love you, *and* when you are so demanding, I feel resentful towards you." The message is left with both parts intact.

An example of a therapeutic movement might sound like this:

> **Client:** *"I resent you making me stay home with you"* (said with a smile).
> **Therapist:** *"Resentful people don't smile. Say it again, feeling it."*
> **C:** *"I resent you making me stay home with you"* (said congruently).
> **T:** *"OK. What's your demand?"*
> **C:** *"I demand that you let me act freely as an adult"* (impassively).
> **T:** *"You don't seem to mean it. Demand it!"*
> **C:** *"I demand that you let me act freely as an adult!"*
> **T:** *"Great! You may get what you want this way. What are you grateful for?"*
> **C:** *"I appreciate you making me stay home with you because you are concerned for my safety, and I know you love me."*

If the client is unable to express the appreciation, have him/her start over with the resentment, showing feelings more honestly. When a client will not allow himself/herself to demand something of a fictitious or absent person, ask for the positive intent behind the reluctance. Then reframe the positive intent and ask the client once again to express the demand.

Integrative Reframe

Situation: Internal conflict exists within a dependent person.
Task: Obtain more resourceful state using integrative reframe.

Step 1   Establish rapport.
      a   Use mirroring techniques.
      b   Validate rapport by leading client.

Step 2   Access inactive state of dependent client's personality.

Step 3   Establish positive framework for state interaction.
      a   Obtain clear commitment to work from this state.
      b   Determine positive intents for being drug free.
      c   Obtain clear commitment to allow the active state to appear and to understand its positive intents.
      d   Ask inactive side to visualize the active side.

Step 4   Have client switch states and step into the picture, inactive to active. Note physiological changes, check for congruence.
      a   Obtain clear commitment to work from this state.
      b   Determine positive intents for early chemical use.

Step 5   Contract with the active state to accomplish its positive intents chemically free.

Step 6   Use appreciative reframe to reconcile positive intents of active and inactive sides, switching states as necessary.

Step 7   Check to see if both sides heard and accepted the appreciation of the other.

Step 8   Contract with each side to work on the other side's positive intents, chemically free.

Step 9   Ask the client to visualize both sides shaking hands, embracing, and becoming one.

Step 10   If a problem occurs here, go back to each side and recheck the acceptance of the other's positive intents.

Step 11   Future pace to check work. If more resourceful physiology occurs, integration is complete.

The final and most complex intervention is the ***integrative reframe***. Once a clinician has developed skills in the previous interventions, this technique is not too difficult.

The clinician must first establish contact and rapport with both the active and inactive sides of the client. Once rapport is established, the clinician should obtain a commitment from each part to let the other part speak and to listen clearly. This should be done congruently from one to the next, regardless of which one is easier to get along with.

To verify your sincerity, move to Step 5 and ask for positive intents. Once these have been acquired from one, switch sides and go through the same exercise.

Switching sides may be accomplished by having the person imagine how he/she would look in a given state—active or inactive. If the person is not sure, ask him/her to act as if he/she knows. If the client is sitting, you might place another chair in front of him/her to allow the sides to switch; or, if standing, you might have the client move from one place to another to role-play the two sides. Be sure to have the two sides facing each other. Note carefully any nonverbal communication the client gives you, because the body will not lie to you regarding the client's congruence with a state.

Once the person has pictured the active side and stepped into the picture, taking on its physiology, you will see a difference in appearance. It is important to make a mental note of what you see, so when the client moves back into the physiology of the inactive state, you will notice the change and can have him/her move to the appropriate physical location.

When you and the client can move freely from one state to the other, use the process of an appreciative reframe to reconcile the state's differences and identify the positive intents of each. Once these positive intents have been identified, it is important to contract with each side that each will help accomplish *the other side's* positive intents, chemically free.

Following the appreciative reframe, there is an opportunity to reframe the concept of chemical urges. Simply contract with both sides to use the feeling of a strong desire for chemicals as an indicator that the "partnership" is not working. This way, the client can perceive such an urge not as a signal to use, and not as a frustrated attempt by the active side to abandon hope, but as a suggestion to get back to work on the combined positive intents.

Throughout this process, if you encounter resistance or refusal from either side, simply go back and identify the positive intents underlying the resistance. The overall goal at this point is awareness, and expressing the positive intents of each side is the best way to make the integrated client aware of all his/her desires.

Once you have this auditory portion of the contract—an agreement or reconciliation between the two sides—then move the client into a visual field. Ask the client to visualize the two parts shaking hands, embracing, and becoming one. Prompt the client to respond verbally, visually, and kinesthetically, so that he/she may experience the moment at all three levels.

Because this work is more involved and complex, it is often more satisfying as well. I have witnessed some remarkable "reunions" and have seen tears of joy fill the eyes of many clients who had previously had nothing but turmoil in their lives. The process of forgiveness comes to fruition as the person reintegrates, and while the reintegration will continue strengthening over a period of months or years, it is often possible to see the client experience new love for himself/herself with the conclusion of this work.

REFERENCE

King, M.L. (1963). *Strength to love.* San Francisco, CA: Collins Publications.

INDEX

ABOUT THE AUTHORS

"From our own awareness we receive many gifts, none of which is greater than to walk our path as we please."

James A. Holder III, MA, has worked in the counseling field for more than 20 years, primarily specializing in addictions treatment. In addition to a bachelor's degree in psychology and a master's degree in counseling, he has received hundreds of hours of training in family counseling, Adlerian psychology, Gestalt Therapy, and Neuro-Linguistic Programming from such trainers as Virginia Satir, John Grinder, Gregory Bateson, and Harold Mosak.

His practical experience is comprehensive: Jim has worked in almost every successful treatment modality—inpatient, outpatient, and residential—in almost every counseling capacity, from service delivery to program direction. As a trainer, Jim has delivered over 800 hours of training to more than 1,000 counseling professionals in a wide variety of disciplines.

An NADAC Level II Credentialed Counselor, Jim has achieved Master Practitioner status in Neuro-Linguistic Programming and Master Counselor's Certification in addictions treatment in South Carolina. He has been on faculty at numerous southeastern schools for alcohol and drug studies.

Jim is now in private practice as a therapist and trainer in Effingham, South Carolina, where he lives with his wife and their two sons.

Thurman Williams III is a free-lance writer who has published extensively in regional and national magazines. He has been involved with addictions treatment since 1985, and is also a successful entrepreneur. He lives with his wife in Columbia, South Carolina.

Introduction to
ALCOHOLISM
COUNSELING:
A Bio-Psycho-Social Approach, Second Edition

Jerome David Levin
New School for Social Research
New York City, New York

"This remarkable book...provides a current and comprehensive discussion of alcoholism for the alcohol counselor and may be the most well written, authoratative, and cogent discussion of this burgeoning and important clinical and public health issue published to date. The material is well organized and so well presented that the book may be read through from 'cover to cover'."
—*Robert B. Millman, M.D., Saul Steinberg Distinguished Professor of Psychiatry and Public Health, Cornell University Medical School, New York City*

Alcoholism counselors must have multiple models — both in research methodology and in psychodynamic formulation — with which to organize and comprehend data. With this in mind, the author has completely updated and expanded material in the second edition of this classic text, complete with an original psychoanalytic model as well as behavioral theories and treatments. It also covers other common, frequently abused drugs to provide a new ideological approach to alcoholism and addiction.

Beginning with the chemical and pharmacological aspects of alcoholism, the book goes on to examine the medical and then the social, anthropological, and psychological underpinnings. In addition to revising these findings and their demographics, there is a broadening of the clinical sections, including comprehensive discussions on traditional treatments and new techniques like acupuncture, biofeedback, and network therapy. Also surveyed are 12-step programs, Alcoholics Anonymous, behavior, dynamic, gestalt, and other counseling styles.

As in the first edition, this remains an informational text, imbuing the reader with an understanding of how various treatment modalities work and what they do best. In addition to its use as a textbook for alcoholism counseling students and as source material for substance abuse counselors, this volume is also accessible to the general reader, the recovering person, and family and friends of both active and recovering alcoholics.

Contents: Preface. Preface to Second Edition. Part 1. Factual. Alcohol: Chemical, Beverage, and Drug. Somatic Illnesses Associated with Alcohol Abuse. How Alcohol Has Been Used. What is Alcoholism? What Do We Know About Alcoholism. Psychological Theories About Alcoholism. Part 2. Treatment. Treatment of Alcoholism. References. Index.

Readership: Substance abuse counselors, students of alcoholism counseling, other health care professionals such as psychologists and social workers, as well as recovering alcoholics and their families, and all other interested individuals.

Taylor & Francis • January 1995 • 225pp • 1-56032-355-8 CL $59.50x • 1-56032-358-2 PB $24.50x

UNDERSTANDING EATING DISORDERS:
Anorexia Nervosa, Bulimia Nervosa, and Obesity

Edited by LeeAnn Alexander-Mott and D. Barry Lumsden,
both of the University of North Texas, Denton

As the incidence of eating disorders such as anorexia nervosa, bulimia nervosa, and obesity (sometimes caused by compulsive eating) has risen, so has research and literature in the field. Presenting current knowledge of these eating disorder—the most common types found in adolescents and adults—this resource addresses issues relevant to all.

Examining the pertinent history, etiology, psychopathology, and sociology, the contributors—all acknowledged authorities in their particular areas—define these eating disorders and discuss issues of recovery and methods of treatment. They also consider the problem as it exists in both males and females in this multicultural society. The resulting volume is divided into four parts: the first gives an overview in general, and the next three focus individually on anorexia nervosa, bulimia nervosa, and obesity respectively.

This will be of interest to those working directly with eating disorders patients— doctors, psychologists, psychiatrists, counselors, nurses, and those working in eating disorder clinics and programs. Teachers and social workers will also find vital information for understanding and dealing with victims of eating disorders.

Contents: 1. General Issues. The Eating Disorders: An Historical Perspective. Critical Issues in the Developmental Psychopathology of Eating Disorders. Parenting and Family Factors in Eating Problems. Sexual Abuse and the Eating Disorders. 2. Anorexia Nervosa: Definition, Diagnostic Criteria, and Associated Psychological Problems; Theories of Etiology; Methods of Treatment. 3. Bulimia Nervosa: Definition, Diagnostic Criteria, and Associated Psychological Problems; Medical Complications; Methods of Treatment. 4. Obesity: Definition, Diagnostic Criteria, and Associated Health Problems; Socio-Cultural Perspectives; Methods of Treatment. Afterword. Index.

Readership: Educators, researchers, students, and other professionals in the field of health care, i.e. psychologists, psychiatrists, doctors, counselors, and social workers; families of eating disorders victims.

Taylor & Francis • August 1994 • 275pp
1-56032-294-2 CL $59.50x • 1-56032-295-0 PB $29.50x

For more information and ordering,
please write or call toll-free:

Taylor & Francis
Publishers since 1798

1900 Frost Road, Suite 101 • Bristol, PA 19007
Phone: 1-800-821-8312

Of similar interest . . .

Academic journals in the social sciences published by Taylor & Francis:

---

*For more
information and ordering,
please write or call:*

Taylor & Francis
1900 Frost Road
Suite 101
Bristol, PA 19007-1598
1-800-821-8312